SMALL PUBLIC LIBRARY
Management

SMALL PUBLIC LIBRARY
Management

JANE PEARLMUTTER & PAUL NELSON

ALA FUNDAMENTALS SERIES

American Library Association : Chicago 2012

Jane Pearlmutter

At the University of Wisconsin–Madison since 1985, Jane Pearlmutter has been responsible for organizing, marketing, and often teaching hundreds of continuing education programs in library and information studies, including core courses for public library director certification and leadership training for state library agencies. She also teaches graduate courses in management and collection development. An active member of the Wisconsin Library Association, Jane has been involved in advocacy and long-range planning for public libraries at the local, state, and national levels.

Paul Nelson

As a department head/assistant director (1978–1986) and library director (1986–2008), Paul Nelson has extensive experience in all aspects of public library administration: governance, advocacy, policy development, budgeting, personnel management, facilities planning, marketing, and long-range planning. Since the mid-1980s, he has provided more than one hundred workshops on these subjects to library systems in the upper Midwest. As Adjunct Assistant Professor at the University of Wisconsin–Madison School of Library and Information Studies, he teaches a reference and information services course and courses in public library management and library advocacy.

© 2012 by the American Library Association

Printed in the United States of America
16 15 14 13 12   5 4 3 2 1

ISBN: 978-0-8389-1085-6 (paper); 978-0-8389-9367-5 (PDF). For more information on digital formats, visit the ALA Store at alastore.ala.org and select eEditions.

Library of Congress Cataloging-in-Publication Data
Pearlmutter, Jane.
  Small public library management / Jane Pearlmutter and Paul Nelson.
     p. cm. — (ALA fundamentals series)
  Includes bibliographical references and index.
  ISBN 978-0-8389-1085-6 (alk. paper)
  1. Small libraries—United States—Administration. 2. Public libraries—United States—Administration. I. Nelson, Paul, 1949– II. Title.
  Z675.S57P43 2012
  025.1'97—dc23
                                                      2011023639

Book design by Casey Bayer in Colaborate and Berkeley. Cover image © moshimochi/Shutterstock, Inc.

♾ This paper meets the requirements of ANSI/NISO Z39.48-1992 (Permanence of Paper).

ALA Editions purchases fund advocacy, awareness, and accreditation programs for library professionals worldwide.

CONTENTS

ACKNOWLEDGMENTS   ix

1 : WHO DO YOU WORK FOR?   1
        The Public Library Defined   1
        Where Are Public Libraries Located?   3
        Administrative Structure and Governance   3
        The Board of Trustees   5
        Working with Local Officials   10
        Library Policy Development   12
        Long-Range Planning   15

2 : LIBRARY FINANCES   21
        Where Does the Money Come From?   21
        Preparing a Budget   30
        Budget Review   35
        Accountability   35
        Terminology   37

3 : PERSONNEL MANAGEMENT   39
        Personnel Policies   40
        Hiring   44
        Personnel Records   46
        Work Schedules   46
        Compensation   47
        Benefits   48
        Supervision   49
        Discipline and Grievances   51
        Volunteers   52

4 : FACILITIES 55

    Defining Library Spaces 55

    Safety Issues 59

    Renovation, Expansion, New Construction 63

    Access to Technology 66

5 : COLLECTION MANAGEMENT 71

    Selection Criteria 73

    Gifts 77

    Circulation Policy 78

    Collection Evaluation, Weeding, and Preservation 79

    Challenges to Library Materials 85

6 : SERVICES AND PROGRAMS 89

    Identifying the Proper Service Mix 89

    Evaluating Services and Programs 96

    Youth Services 97

    Adult Services 98

    Reference Services 100

    Readers' Advisory 104

    Technology and Library Service 105

    Classes and Informal Instruction 106

    Outreach Services 109

    Community Use of Library Spaces 111

    Promoting Services and Programs 115

7 : THE LIBRARY AS PLACE 123

    Developing a Community-Centered Philosophy 123

    Library Advocacy 126

    Keeping Up with Library Issues 132

INDEX 135

ACKNOWLEDGMENTS

FIRST ATTRIBUTED TO University of Wisconsin President Charles Van Hise in 1904, the Wisconsin Idea is the principle that education should influence and improve people's lives beyond the university classroom. Out of this background, a continuing education program for librarians began in Wisconsin over fifty years ago. In 1971, when certification for Wisconsin public library directors became mandatory, the required courses for directors in small communities were offered via correspondence and via the state's Educational Telephone Network. This dedicated, audio-only network seems very primitive today, but it provided the means to deliver courses to every county and gave small-town librarians an opportunity to share experiences, tips, and questions. Wisconsin's early approach to distance education eventually evolved into online courses, and we'd like to thank the UW–Madison School of Library and Information Studies for maintaining its commitment to continuing education for staff in small public libraries, and the Wisconsin Department of Public Instruction, Division for Libraries, Technology, and Community Learning for funding the development of the online course in basic library management for small libraries. Teaching these certification courses in library management, reference, and collection development has provided us with the opportunity to work with hundreds of librarians in small public libraries (many of whom began their positions with no formal library education and little exposure to library management), and that experience has made this book possible. We gratefully acknowledge our colleagues in small libraries (including many of our former students) who generously contributed their stories and examples to this book.

CHAPTER ONE

WHO DO YOU WORK FOR?

THE PUBLIC LIBRARY DEFINED

Ask a random group of people to describe a public library, and you are likely to receive a wide variety of responses. One person may appreciate the variety of print and audiovisual materials that are available for loan. Another person may feel he'd be lost without the library's public access Internet computers to keep him connected with family and friends in distant locations. Parents of small children may point to the importance of storytimes and family programs. By the time a dozen people have offered their perspectives, they'll have created a varied and detailed picture of the informational, educational, recreational, and cultural needs of the community that the library meets. From these interviews, we can obtain a subjective definition of a public library—what this vital agency means to an individual.

As the federal agency responsible for collecting, organizing, and disseminating statistics at the national level, the Institute of Museum and Library Services provides us with a concise, objective, five-point definition of a "public library":

> A public library is . . . established under state enabling laws or regulations to serve a community, district, or region, and . . . provides at least the following:
>
> 1. An organized collection of printed or other library materials, or a combination thereof;
>
> 2. Paid staff;
>
> 3. An established schedule in which services of the staff are available to the public;

4. The facilities necessary to support such a collection, staff, and schedule; and . . .

5. Is supported in whole or in part with public funds. [1]

This definition of a public library conveniently highlights the subject coverage in subsequent chapters of this book: financial management and recordkeeping, personnel management, facilities, collections, and services and programs.

Highlights in U.S. Library History

1816 First state library. Pennsylvania creates a state library agency by merging the collections of the Senate, House, and Assembly. The position of State Librarian is officially designated.

1833 First free public library. Established in Peterborough, New Hampshire, the library is maintained by a public tax, controlled and managed by town vote, and open to all community members without restriction.

1849 First free libraries authorized by a state. The New Hampshire legislature authorizes the creation of public libraries *"open to the free use of every inhabitant."*

1859 First library newspaper room. The Cooper Union for the Advancement of Science and Art offers twenty-eight daily newspapers in a reading room of just over 10,000 square feet. Open from 8 a.m. to 10 p.m., the reading room is "free to all persons of good moral character for the use and instruction of the working classes."

1887 First library school. Melvil Dewey establishes the world's first library school at Columbia College (now Columbia University).

1889 First children's department. Minneapolis Public Library separates children's books from the rest of the collection. A separate room is set aside in 1892.

1898 First county library. Van Wert County, Ohio, establishes Brumback Library. New building opens in 1901. Funds are provided through a county tax levy.

1905 First traveling library. The Washington County Free Library in Hagerstown, Maryland, refits a former grocery wagon with bookshelves. The wagon follows a schedule of stops throughout the county three times a week.

1956 First federal aid to libraries. Congress authorizes the Library Services Act "to promote the further development of public library service in rural areas."

1968 First online library database. The Machine Readable Cataloging System (MARC) is developed by a computer programmer for the Library of Congress.

1971 First computerized library network. OCLC, the Ohio College Library Center, is established at Ohio State University by the Ohio College Association, a consortium of fifty-four academic libraries.

1996 First online library provided by a state. DelAWARE, the Digital Library of the First State, offers links to numerous databases, reference texts, archives, and periodicals. Accessible to any resident with a current library card.

Source: Adapted from Joseph Nathan Kane, *Famous First Facts*, 6th edition (New York: H. W. Wilson, 2007).

WHERE ARE PUBLIC LIBRARIES LOCATED?

In 2007, the 9,214 public libraries in the United States served 97 percent of the total population, a figure that has remained steady for more than a decade. As shown in table 1.1, the majority of these libraries (88 percent) are located in small cities and villages with a legal service population of less than 50,000. Large public libraries may serve the majority of Americans, nearly 75 percent, but it is the small public library that has the larger number of outlets. The population service area of more than half of U.S. public libraries is less than 10,000.[2]

ADMINISTRATIVE STRUCTURE AND GOVERNANCE

In very general terms, public libraries in the United States are legally established under local or state law in one of three ways (see table 1.2):[3]

TABLE 1.1 : **Percentage and number of U.S. public libraries by population group**

Population	% of Total	Total number
Less than 1,000	11.60	1,072
1,000 to 2,499	16.50	1,524
2,500 to 4,999	14.50	1,340
5,000 to 9,999	16.10	1,483
10,000 to 24,999	19.10	1,764
25,000 to 49,999	10.30	952
50,000 to 99,999	6.00	556
100,000 to 249,999	3.60	335
250,000 to 499,999	1.10	104
500,000 to 999,999	0.60	58
1,000,000 or more	0.30	26
Total	100.00	9,214

Source: Institute of Museum and Library Services, *Public Libraries Survey: Fiscal Year 2007.*

1. *Single direct service outlet.* An administrative entity that serves the public directly with one central library, books-by-mail-only, or one bookmobile. (In the 2007 Institute of Museum and Library Services *Public Libraries Survey,* 81 percent of all U.S. public libraries fall into this category, as do 96.5 percent of libraries with a service area population of less than 10,000.)

2. *Multiple direct service outlets where administrative offices are not separate.* An administrative entity that serves the public directly with two or more service outlets, including some combination of one central library, branch(es), bookmobile(s), and/or books-by-mail-only (17.6 percent of U.S. public libraries fall into this category).

3. *Multiple direct service outlets where administrative offices are separate.* An administrative entity that serves the public directly with two or more service outlets, including some combination of one central library, branch(es), bookmobile(s), and/or books-by-mail-only. The administrative offices are separate from the direct service outlets (1.4 percent of U.S. public libraries are in this category).

Governance is also divided into categories. For its reporting purposes, the Institute of Museum and Library Services organizes public library governance structures into the following groups:[4]

1. *Municipal government.* A public library is authorized to operate within the structure of a city or village government. (In 2007, 52.8 percent of U.S. public libraries were organized in this manner.)

2. *County or parish.* A public library operates within the structure of a county or parish government (9.9 percent of U.S. public libraries in 2007).

TABLE 1.2 : Percentage of U.S. libraries by type of administrative structure and population of legal service area

Population	Single outlet (%)	Multiple outlets, administration not separate (%)	Multiple outlets, administration separate (%)
Total	81.0	17.6	1.4
Less than 1,000	99.8	0.2	0.0
1,000 to 2,499	98.5	1.5	0.0
2,500 to 4,999	97.4	2.6	0.0
5,000 to 9,999	92.0	7.8	0.1
10,000 to 24,999	81.3	18.2	0.5
25,000 to 49,999	62.4	36.1	1.5
50,000 to 99,999	30.2	66.4	3.4
100,000 to 249,999	6.9	82.4	10.7
250,000 to 499,999	1.9	81.7	16.3
500,000 to 999,999	0.0	67.2	32.8
1,000,000 or more	0.0	61.5	38.5

Source: Institute of Museum and Library Services, *Public Libraries Survey: Fiscal Year 2007.*

3. *City/county.* A public library is a multijurisdictional entity operated jointly by a city and county (1.2 percent of U.S. public libraries in 2007).

4. *Multijurisdictional.* A public library is operated jointly by two or more units of local government under an intergovernmental agreement (3.4 percent of U.S. public libraries in 2007).

5. *Nonprofit association or agency libraries.* A public library is privately controlled but meets the statutory definition of a public library in a given state. (In 2007, 14.8 percent of U.S. public libraries. A majority or plurality of public libraries in Maine, New York, Pennsylvania, and Rhode Island are organized in this manner.)

6. *School district.* A public library is under the jurisdiction of a school district (2.0 percent of U.S. public libraries in 2007).

7. *Public library district.* As an independent taxing authority, a local entity other than a county, municipality, township, or school district is authorized by state law to establish and operate a public library. (In 2007, 14.5 percent of U.S. public libraries. The majority of public libraries in Delaware, Idaho, Illinois, Kentucky, and Missouri are organized in this manner.)

8. *Other.* This category includes Native American tribal government and combined public/school libraries, as well as the public libraries of Hawaii, which are operated under a single state agency, the Department of Education (2.0 percent of U.S. public libraries in 2007).

THE BOARD OF TRUSTEES

Although there is no single standard of public library governance, the majority of public libraries in the United States, small libraries in particular, are organized as part of a municipal government. In almost all cases, though, the library is governed by an independent board of trustees, usually appointed but sometimes elected (as in the case of public library districts), with clearly defined, statutory responsibilities.

Although specific responsibilities may vary from state to state, a board of trustees is generally accountable for three general areas of the library's operations:

- appointing a librarian and supervising the administration of the library
- adopting an annual budget and providing financial oversight
- determining and adopting written policies to govern the operation and programs of the library

In addition, board members need to be strong and visible advocates for the library in the community, engage in long-range planning activities, and monitor and evaluate the overall effectiveness of the library's operation.

Library boards are typically made up of citizen representatives who are residents of the community or service area and who share three important traits:

- genuine interest in the library as an essential service
- familiarity with the community
- general knowledge of library policies and procedures

Citizen representation is critical for a number of reasons. First, it helps to isolate the library from political pressure. Second, it ensures that a library's collection reflects all points of view and that efforts to remove or limit access to materials are strongly resisted. Last, a citizen board means that the library is governed by the same people it serves—the public. In some instances, though, state law requires the appointment of specific representatives to the library board, such as a city council or village board liaison or the school district superintendent or a designee. State and local situations may vary, and service area population may be a factor, but generally five to nine members may serve on a library board.

Most library board members are appointed by a mayor, city manager, county executive, or other similar official. These appointments are then forwarded to the municipality's or county's governmental body for approval. Library directors have a role to play in this process through recruitment, an effort to find people who are willing to serve and who have the best interests of the library as their top priority. This task can be accomplished in several ways, including through direct contact or by developing an application form. Mayors and county executives are usually pleased to receive the names of volunteers to serve on the many boards, committees, and commissions to which they make appointments. Without this extra step in library board development of seeking out potential members, a director may end up with an appointee uninterested in or unsuitable for the assignment.

LIBRARY BOARD BYLAWS

In order to function effectively, a library board must establish the rules that govern its activities. These rules are codified in its bylaws. At a minimum, this document should specify the election of officers, scheduling of meetings, appointments to committees, and the process by which bylaws are amended.

Most boards elect a president, vice president, secretary, and treasurer, a process initiated with the president's appointment of a nominating committee. The "Officers" article of the bylaws describes how they are elected and lists the responsibilities assigned to each officer. Term limits and procedures for filling vacancies are also addressed in this section.

The article on "Meetings" sets regular and annual meeting dates, describes the posting of agendas and other notices, notes the conditions for the scheduling of special meetings, and establishes a quorum—that is, the number of members that must be present in order to conduct official business. All meetings should be held in compliance with any open meetings laws and follow the rules of parliamentary procedure.

Depending on the needs and workload of the board, the president may appoint a number of standing committees, which is typically done in the areas of personnel, budget, building, and policy. Ad hoc committees are formed to study a specific issue or problem, such as long-range planning or technology, and may include staff, public representatives, and outside experts. An ad hoc committee is generally given a deadline for completing its report, at which time the group is dissolved. Committees of the board are advisory in nature. In other words, it is the responsibility of the full board to take action on specific recommendations.

Board members must abide by a code of ethics in the commission of their duties. For this reason, bylaws should address potential conflicts of interest, such as a member acting as a private citizen in negotiations with the public library over a contract in which he or she has a direct or indirect financial interest. A board member should withdraw from any discussions, deliberations, and votes that have a whiff of special interest.

THE RELATIONSHIP BETWEEN THE LIBRARY BOARD AND THE LIBRARY DIRECTOR

The partnership between board and director works best when their separate roles and responsibilities are clearly understood and mutually respected. While the board is primarily responsible for the big picture (determining the service program, setting policy, having financial oversight), the director administers the day-to-day operations of the library (preparing reports, managing the collection, supervising other staff). The board must give the director a certain degree of autonomy in decision making. For example, if state law gives the board the authority to "audit

---

An Invitation to Serve Your Library

The library depends on citizen involvement to ensure that its services are as reflective of community needs as possible.

The _____ Public Library Board of Trustees is a [9]-member board appointed by the mayor. As a policy-making body, it guides the development of library services. Terms on the board are [three years]. The board meets on the [day or week and time, e.g., second Tuesday of each month at 6:30 p.m.].

Effective trustees bring to the library a knowledge of the community, a commitment to the rights of citizens to information, and a willingness to continually maintain and strengthen library services.

If you are interested in serving on the Library Board, please complete the form below and return it to the Library Director. This expression of interest will make your name available for consideration by the mayor at the time of a vacancy but will not, of course, guarantee appointment. For more information, please contact Library Director at [phone number] or [e-mail].

Thank you for your interest in the library.

Name _____

E-mail _____

Address _____ Phone _____

Education _____

_____

Work/volunteer experience _____

_____

Skills/expertise that you can bring to the board _____

_____

_____

Source: Middleton (Wisconsin) Public Library.

Public Library Board of Trustees Job Description

References: Municipal Ordinances, Chapter _____; State Statutes, Chapter _____

Legal Responsibilities
Members of the library board are mandated by [state] law to control

- Library funds
- Library property
- Library expenditures
- Selection and hiring of a library director

Members of the library board are required to maintain open records and hold open meetings under the requirements of Chapter _____ of the State Statutes.

Fiduciary Responsibilities
Public library trustees are public officers and therefore have a responsibility to:

- Obey federal, state, county, and local laws as they relate to libraries
- Conform practices to board bylaws
- Manage all library assets wisely
- Recognize that the library's best interests must prevail over any individual interest
- Ensure adequate recordkeeping and documentation

Examples of Duties

- Select, hire, and supervise a qualified library director.
- Determine and adopt written policies to govern the operation and program of the library.
- Develop a long-range plan to meet the changing needs of the service population.
- Adopt an annual budget adequate for meeting goals and objectives; work actively for public and official support of the budget.
- Review monthly financial statements; approve reasonable expenditures that are within the approved budget; forward approved bills for payment by county.
- Negotiate, approve, and enter into contracts for services.
- Develop and maintain capital improvement plan.
- Establish, support, and participate in a planned public relations program.

Qualifications for Library Trustees

- Willingness to devote time and talents
- Ability to think clearly, question objectively, and plan creatively
- Skill in communicating and cooperating
- Awareness and appreciation of the library's past, present, and future role in society
- Willingness to become more knowledgeable about library services and standards of operation
- Ability to represent the Library Board and advocate for libraries in public forums

Collectively, the Library Board of Trustees should represent:

- A diversity of interests
- A balance of age, race, sex, and socioeconomic levels
- A variety of occupational and personal backgrounds
- A diversity of geographic areas within the Public Library's service area

Source: Middleton (Wisconsin) Public Library; adapted from Dane County (Wisconsin) Library ServiceTex.

and approve all vouchers for the expenditures of the public library," this language should not be interpreted to require that the director justify each purchase individually.

Table 1.3 clarifies the duties of the library board and library director in specific areas of shared responsibility.

TABLE 1.3 : Duties of the library board and the library director

	Library Board	Library Director
Bylaws	Adopt bylaws for board procedures.	Develop and review bylaws in consultation with board.
Staff	Employ a competent and qualified director. Review the director's organizational structure, identifying lines of authority and responsibility.	Act as technical advisor to the board. Employ and supervise all other staff members. Make recommendations on organizational structure to the board.
Policy	Determine and adopt written policies to govern the operation and program of the library.	Recommend and draft policies for board action. Carry out adopted policies, delegating responsibilities to staff as needed.
Planning/ capital projects	In cooperation with director and staff, develop a long-range plan for commitment of resources to meet the changing needs of the community.	Work together with board and staff in preparation of a long-range plan by projecting needs and trends in library service.
Budget	Review the annual budget to determine its adequacy for meeting goals and objectives. Work actively for public and official support. Explore all possible revenue sources.	Prepare the annual budget draft to achieve objectives as identified with the board. Supply facts and figures to aid in interpreting the library's financial needs. Attend budget hearings as a resource person.
Finance	Review and approve monthly financial statements in context of the annual budget.	Prepare and present monthly financial statements and bills for board action.
Public relations	Establish, support, and participate in a planned public relations program. Interpret the library's role and plans to other community boards and committees.	Maintain an active program of public relations and public information. Represent the library on other community boards and committees.
Library legislation	Know local and state laws. Actively support state and national library legislation.	Know local and state laws. Keep board informed of pending legislation, library trends, developments, and standards.
Advocacy	Report regularly to governing officials and the general public.	Report regularly to the library board, local government officials, the general public, and the state library agency.

Source: Adapted from Middleton (Wisconsin) Public Library (1986).

Building Effective Working Relationships with Your Board: Dos and Don'ts

Do

- Provide information in a concise format and timely manner (agendas, reports, proposals).
- Encourage, don't force, all board members to participate in discussions at meetings.
- Confer with board president prior to each meeting to review agenda.
- Meet with new board members, provide them with appropriate background materials, and give them a tour before their first meeting.

Don't

- Arrive late or unprepared for a meeting. (The same, of course, can be said for board members.)
- Speak in library jargon.
- Spring any surprises, such as asking board members to act on a proposal or recommendation as you distribute it to them.
- Overwhelm board members with operational details, particularly if the issue is outside their primary areas of responsibility.

WORKING WITH LOCAL OFFICIALS

The best way to work with local officials is to start at the beginning. Within the first month on a new job, a library director should make individual appointments with those elected and appointed officials—council members, county board supervisors, township supervisors, city and county administrators—who represent or serve the library's service area. It's a major commitment of time but well worth the effort in the long run. Building relationships with local officials should be an element of every library director's position description. It's the most effective way to ensure that the library has "a place at the table" when budget, policy, and planning discussions occur at the municipal or county level.

Where should these one-on-one meetings take place? At the library, of course.

The first order of business is a tour of the facility, a strategy that may help to reinforce concerns about space needs, collection development, staffing, or other high-priority issues. The official should be given the opportunity to see all areas of the library: public, staff, meeting rooms, storage. This approach provides the best impact when the tour is scheduled during a peak time of library use.

When the tour has been completed, the conversation continues in the director's office. By the time the meeting concludes, the following points will have been well covered.

The director shares his or her philosophy of library service—in essence, anticipating the question, "Why is a public library an essential service in our community?"

The director describes what he or she hopes to accomplish over the long term (e.g., a building program, new or expanded services or both, technology needs).

When asked, officials share the reasons why they chose to serve the municipality or county in their current capacity. ("What made you decide to run for the [council, county board]?" The answer to this question may allow the director to learn if a particular official has a big-picture view or a narrow-interest agenda.)

When asked, officials share their sense of the community's or county's priorities. ("What are the most important issues facing the city/county over the next few years?" A follow-up question is in order if an official does not mention libraries unprompted.)

An important outcome of this process is that the library director becomes known to officials on a first-name basis and not just by a generic job title. In addition, the director learns how the library is perceived by officials in the overall municipal or county picture. Most importantly, though, the meetings serve as an effective way to identify the library's allies and adversaries and are important building blocks in a program of library advocacy.

Once the initial series of meetings has been conducted, the director continues this process on at least an annual basis. In other words, after each spring, fall, or special election, newly elected officials are invited to the library for a tour and informal discussion. The ultimate benefit of this meeting cycle is that the library director provides officials with a clear sense of the library's mission and goals and is not just seen as someone pleading for money at budget time.

GETTING OUT THE LIBRARY MESSAGE:
A Checklist for the Director, Board Members, and Designated Staff

Municipality
- Mayor
- City administrator
- Council members
- Members of personnel and finance committees
- Department heads

County
- Executive (or Chief of Staff)
- Board supervisors
- Members of personnel and finance committees

Township
- Chair
- Supervisors

School District
- Superintendent
- School board president
- School librarians
- Reading specialists

Chamber of Commerce
- Executive director
- Chair, board of directors

LIBRARY POLICY DEVELOPMENT

Policies provide the framework for a library's operations. They guide the decision-making process of the board, director, and staff and give a clear sense of organization to the library's ongoing activities. Policies in the areas of circulation, public access computers, and meeting rooms, for example, promote the effective use of library resources. Policies also provide the guarantee that all library users will be treated fairly and equally.

Library policies fall into two categories. External policies (circulation, reference, programming) determine how the library serves the public. Internal policies (personnel, volunteers, responsibilities of staff when the director is absent) govern library board operations and library management.

Procedures, on the other hand, are defined as the steps required to complete a specific task, such as registering a person for a library card. A circulation policy, for example, will set forth who is eligible to apply for a card and what type of identification is required but should not include a detailed description of everything a patron and staff member must do to complete the process. Many libraries develop a separate procedures manual for use in staff training (see table 1.4).

Policy development and review should be a "bottom-up" process: public input, staff, director, and board. From a practical standpoint, frontline staff members at the circulation desk, for example, are going to have the best sense as to how a policy addressing loan periods, overdues, and renewals are perceived by library users. Once a staff review has taken place, the director submits a draft policy to the library board for discussion, revision, and approval.

As the review team, the library board is responsible for ensuring that policies contain legal, clear, and reasonable language. State law, for example, might preclude public libraries

---

TABLE 1.4 : Is it policy or is it procedure?

Policy	Procedure
Has library-wide application.	Has narrow application, usually specific to work flow within a department or area of the library.
Describes in broad terms the operational framework in which the library operates.	Describes in detail the specific tasks required to complete a task (e.g., processing library materials).
Addresses the issues of "what" and "why."	Addresses the issue of "how."
Is flexible enough in some cases to allow supervisors to use their discretion.	Is less flexible due to the need to follow a prescribed series of steps to complete a task successfully.
Changes infrequently and must be approved by library board.	Changes frequently and is informally agreed to by the staff involved.

from charging for services, including Internet access and interlibrary loan. Any fees applied to these services would not conform to current law and would, therefore, be illegal. If people are banned from the library for engaging in "inappropriate behavior," clear definitions of this behavior must be specified. Restricting certain types of activities (no talking, no crying babies) is likely to be unenforceable—that is, unreasonable—at certain times of the day. The board must also support the staff's efforts to enforce all policies fairly and without discrimination. No favoritism, in other words.

Before a new or revised policy is implemented, library staff members need to build awareness of any impending changes. For example, long waits for public access Internet computers may result in the need to enforce stricter time limits. Signs announcing this policy change should be posted in appropriate locations.

As the person responsible for administering board-approved policies, the director incorporates development and review as ongoing activities. To stay current, all policies should be reviewed on a three-year cycle. In addition, the director encourages staff and public input on an ongoing basis, promotes and publicizes policies with local officials and other community leaders, and ensures that policies are implemented in a consistent manner among all staff members.

POLICY CHECKLIST

The scope of a library's policy development is dependent upon the breadth of its service program and the amenities its facility provides. What follows is a checklist of standard policies. Specific issues of policy development are discussed in subsequent chapters.

Appropriate behavior. Although by design this type of policy contains some restrictions, its overall purpose is intended to be positive. It sets forth the library's commitment to providing an atmosphere where people of all ages and circumstances feel welcome and safe.

Bulletin board (public notices). Most libraries provide space for the display of public notices of events and services of a cultural, educational, or community nature.

Circulation. This policy ensures equal access for all to the library's materials and services. At the same time, it ensures that some borrowers don't abuse their privileges to the detriment of others. In an era of increased resource sharing, agreements with other libraries and consortia should be referenced and their benefits briefly explained.

Collection development. This critical policy is used by library staff to select, maintain, preserve, and weed materials. It can also serve as a tool to acquaint the public with the principles of collection development and intellectual freedom.

Emergency/disaster. Policy development in these areas requires close coordination with municipal and county governments and staff training to ensure a proper response during an emergency.

Exhibits. Many libraries provide space for the display of educational and cultural exhibits provided by local, state, and national organizations.

Gifts. At a minimum, a gift policy must clearly state that a library will accept books, audiovisual materials, and any other items with the understanding that the board has the authority to use or dispose of them however it sees fit.

Group visits and tours. Libraries encourage group visits and tours on a scheduled basis to promote their materials, programs, and services. Such visits and tours, however, should not interfere with the library's operations.

Internet use. The Internet is now an integral part of a library's service program in helping people find the information they need. Policy development in this area should not be overlooked.

Meeting rooms/study rooms. In most cases, meeting rooms are used primarily for the library's own programs. When otherwise available, they may be booked by local and area groups for programs and meetings, subject to the guidelines set forth by the library board.

Personnel. The hiring, training, supervision, motivation, and evaluation of staff are key factors in developing high-quality library service. A personnel policy provides the framework for creating a positive workplace environment.

Programs (library-sponsored). An increasingly popular feature, programs for all ages promote library materials, facilities, and services as well as offering the community an informational, entertaining, or cultural experience.

Reference. This policy addresses the three main aspects of providing reference services: personal assistance by staff, formal and informal instruction in the use of library resources, and access to a wide range of information through print and online resources and the use of interlibrary loan and document delivery networks.

Responsibility for library operations. This type of policy is particularly important in libraries without an assistant director position.

Volunteers. Volunteers enhance, rather than replace, library staffing. They allow the library to make the best use of its fiscal resources and help connect it to other community groups and organizations.

The Four Outcomes of Successful Policy Development

Builds knowledge. Increases staff members' understanding of the library's mission.

Eliminates confusion. Allows staff to answer the question, "What do I do in this situation?" without consulting a supervisor.

Reduces frustration. Keeps staff in the loop. "Nobody told me about this" is no longer an operative excuse.

Lowers stress. Allows staff to approach their work with confidence.

LONG-RANGE PLANNING

Planning for library services is one of the most important shared responsibilities of a library board and library director. A clear, concise, and credible planning document provides the community with a road map to the library's development. It distills the vision of what the board and staff hope to accomplish during a specific time period, usually three to five years. Most importantly, it describes the goals, objectives, activities, and outcomes within each selected service area and provides a step-by-step account of how the library will achieve this vision.

Long-range planning is a formal, ongoing visioning process that involves the library board, library staff, city officials, municipal or county employees (or both), and representatives from community groups and organizations (especially those with whom the library has partnerships) as well as library users and nonusers. In essence, it asks participants to answer the following basic questions about the library and its place in the community.

- Where are we?
- Where do we want to go?
- How do we get there?

Depending upon the scope of the process, a library board may hire a consultant to guide the participants through their deliberations. In most cases, though, the library director serves as the project coordinator, although the concept of using a volunteer facilitator for certain planning activities has gained traction in recent years.

LIBRARY SERVICE ROLES AND RESPONSES

Since 1980, the American Library Association has published a series of guidebooks for long-range planning. The earliest compilation, *A Planning Process for Public Libraries,* provides a comprehensive overview of procedures and activities. A follow-up volume published in 1987, *Planning and Role Setting for Public Libraries: A Manual of Options and Procedures,* attempts to streamline the process and presents a menu of eight public library service roles from which libraries are encouraged to choose to focus their planning efforts. A 1998 revision, *Planning for Results: A Public Library Transformation Process,* presents a visioning element that encourages participants to look beyond the library itself and design a plan in which the community benefits from a strong, well-supported program of library services for all ages and circumstances. *Strategic Planning for Results* (2008) and its companion volume, *Implementing for Results: Your Strategic Plan in Action* (2009), titles in the PLA Results Series, provide a menu of eighteen service responses, areas in which public libraries may choose to develop specific elements of their service program (see table 1.5).

THE PLANNING TIME LINE

The latest version of the planning model takes the commitment factor into consideration by reducing the amount of time required to complete the entire process—from nine to four months[5]—as summarized in table 1.6.

THE PLANNING DOCUMENT

At a minimum, the written long-range plan will cover the following five areas:

1. *Title page.* At a glance, the document must show a clear connection to the library whose goals and objectives it presents. Include the plan's date of approval and the time period it covers.

2. *Introduction or executive summary.* The board president or library director summarizes the purpose of the document and the process that led to the publication of the committee's results. This section may also contain a brief statement regarding the library's essential role in the community and highlight the major goals and anticipated outcomes.

3. *Mission statement.* "Why do we have a library?" A mission statement answers this question by providing a succinct description of the library's purpose and lists the ways in which this mission will be accomplished.

Public Library Service Roles

Although these service roles were introduced more than twenty years ago, many small public libraries still use them as a way to set priorities in the development of a long-range planning document. They are a more manageable alternative to the comprehensive list of eighteen public library service responses. The most commonly selected service roles are Preschoolers' Door to Learning, Popular Materials Center, and Reference Library.

Community Activities Center. The library is a central focus point for community activities, meetings, and services.

Community Information Center. The library is a clearinghouse for current information on community organizations, issues, and services.

Formal Education Support Center. The library assists students of all ages in meeting educational objectives established during their formal courses of study.

Independent Learning Center. The library supports individuals of all ages pursuing a sustained program of learning independent of any educational provider.

Popular Materials Center. The library features current, high-demand, high-interest materials in a variety of formats for persons of all ages.

Preschoolers' Door to Learning. The library encourages young children to develop an interest in reading and learning through services for children and for parents and children together.

Reference Library. The library actively provides timely, accurate, and useful information to community residents.

Research Center. The library assists scholars and researchers to conduct in-depth studies, investigate specific areas of knowledge, and create new knowledge.

Source: Charles R. McClure, Amy Owen, Douglas L. Zweizig, Mary Jo Lynch, and Nancy A. Van House, *Planning and Role Setting for Public Libraries: A Manual of Options and Procedures*, prepared for the Public Library Development Project (Chicago: American Library Association, 1987).

TABLE 1.5 : Public library service responses

Service response	What is addressed	What the library provides
Be an informed citizen	Local, national, and world affairs	Information to support and promote democracy, to fulfill civic responsibilities at all levels, and to participate in community decision making
Build successful enterprises	Business and nonprofit support	Tools to develop and maintain strong, viable organizations
Celebrate diversity	Cultural awareness	Programs and services that promote understanding and appreciation of cultural heritages
Connect to the online world	Public Internet access	High-speed access to the digital world with no unnecessary restrictions or fees
Create young readers	Early literacy	Preschool programs and services designed to ensure children will be ready to learn to read, write, and listen when they enter school
Discover your roots	Genealogy and local history	Resources to connect the past with the present through family histories and to understand the history and traditions of the community
Express creativity	Create and share content	Services and support to create original print, video, audio, or visual content in a real-world or online environment
Get facts fast	Ready reference	Someone to answer questions on a wide array of topics of personal interest
Know your community	Community resources and services	Central source for information about the programs, services, and activities provided by community agencies and organizations
Learn to read and write	Adult, teen, and family literacy	Support to improve literacy skills in order to meet personal goals and fulfill responsibilities as parents, citizens, and workers
Make career choices	Job and career development	Resources to identify and select career options related to individual strengths and interests
Make informed decisions	Health, wealth, and other life choices	Resources to identify and analyze risks, benefits, and alternatives before making decisions
Satisfy curiosity	Lifelong learning	Resources to explore topics of personal interest
Stimulate imagination	Reading, viewing, and listening for pleasure	Accessible materials in sufficient numbers selected to enhance leisure time
Succeed in school	Homework help	Resources for students to succeed in school
Understand how to find, evaluate, and use information	Information fluency	Information to resolve an issue or answer a question and the skills to locate, evaluate, and effectively use information
Visit a comfortable place	Physical and virtual spaces	A safe and welcoming physical place to meet and interact with others or to sit quietly and read, and open and accessible virtual spaces that support social networking
Welcome to the United States	Services for immigrants	Information on citizenship, English language learning, employment, public schooling, social services, and other topics to participate successfully in American life

Source: Adapted from Sandra Nelson, *Implementing for Results: Your Strategic Plan in Action* (Chicago: American Library Association, 2009).

TABLE 1.6 : Planning time line

Time line	Task	Steps to completion
Month 1	Design the planning process.	• Identify reasons for planning. • Define planning responsibilities. • Prepare planning budget and schedule. • Develop communication plan. • Design and present staff orientation.
Month 1	Start the planning process.	• Obtain board approval. • Select community planning committee members. • Invite committee members. • Prepare and distribute community and library information packets.
Month 1	Identify community needs.	• Present an orientation to planning committee. • Develop community vision statements. • Define current conditions in community. • Decide what needs to be done to reach community vision.
Month 2	Select service responses.	• Present overview of library to community members. • Select preliminary service responses. • Describe effect of preliminary service responses on current library services. • Select final service responses.
Month 2	Prepare for change.	• Assess the library's readiness for change. • Plan to create positive environment for change. • Review and revise communications plan. • Train supervisors and managers.
Month 2	Consider library values and mission.	• Define values. • Consider the library mission.
Month 3	Write goals and objectives.	• Write service response goals. • Write service response objectives. • Determine priority of goals and measures of progress for each unit.
Month 3	Identify organizational competencies.	• Understand organizational competencies and initiatives. • Identify organizational issues. • Write organization competencies and initiatives.
Month 4	Write the strategic plan, obtain approval.	• Write and review the strategic plan. • Submit the strategic plan for approval.
Month 4	Communicate the results of the planning process.	• Define the target audiences. • Develop a communications plan. • Develop communications to target audiences.

Source: Sandra S. Nelson, *Strategic Planning for Libraries* (Chicago: American Library Association, 2008).

4. *Goals and objectives.* Each goal and objective agreed upon by the planning committee and approved by the library board should be included. They can be arranged in priority order or categorized by the service responses the library has chosen to emphasize. Selected examples of activities should be included to demonstrate how the goals and objectives will be achieved.

5. *Evaluation.* The document concludes with a brief statement about the ongoing nature of the planning process and how progress toward reaching goals and objectives will be measured.

COLLECTING DATA

In creating a long-range plan and administering the day-to-day business of the library, a director needs access to accurate, valid data to guide the decision-making process and to present officials with examples of the effectiveness of the library's service program. In very general terms, one subset of this data provides a current statistical overview of the library's internal operations as well as the service area's demographics. An equally important subset is the data developed by and for governments, schools, and businesses that attempts to predict future growth patterns and development. The director collects and analyzes this data to serve a number of purposes: planning, budget development, promotion, and advocacy.

Computerized library systems generate a wealth of useful statistics for library planning and evaluation. These numbers give the staff a sense of how the collection is being used—both in general terms (circulation of adult, teen, and children's materials) and within specific Dewey decimal classifications. In the latter case, for example, collection development staff can identify those subject areas where there is increased activity and adjust their purchasing patterns accordingly. Statistics may also be generated to determine library use by day of the week or

---

Mission Statement

The mission of the Middleton Public Library is to make a positive difference in the quality of life in our community.

We will accomplish our mission by . . .

- Advocating for the importance of free access to knowledge, information, and the diversity of ideas.
- Defending Wisconsin's 130-year tradition of free and open access to public libraries.
- Meeting the educational, information, and recreational needs of the community through access to traditional and nontraditional library resources.
- Providing highly competent staff who work together with the library board and city officials to develop and implement clearly focused and shared goals.
- Offering a safe and welcoming environment in an aesthetically pleasing and conveniently organized facility.

Source: Middleton (Wisconsin) Public Library (2004).

hour of the day. In addition, creating spreadsheets that gather circulation statistics over a five- or ten-year period allows staff to identify trends.

As for demographic and other community information, this data ought to be right at a director's fingertips. Here are some examples.

U.S. Census Bureau (www.census.gov). People and households: estimates, projections, housing, income.

All fifty states provide a wealth of statistical information classified by counties and municipalities (population, education, health, business, and more) via their official websites.

County government is another useful source for data collection, particularly in the areas of regional trends, labor market conditions, and analyses of federal census data.

Most municipalities generate considerable statistical information and planning documents of their own. Examples of these include community profiles, comprehensive development plans, environmental assessments, traffic management plans, and planning agreements with neighboring municipalities. (If these or similar documents are not available online, the director should request a copy for the library's reference collection.)

School districts collect data on current demographics (population, race/ethnicity, poverty, disabilities) and long-range planning (residential development; enrollment history, trends, and projections). Useful information regarding the curriculum may also be obtained: academic and technology standards, library selection policies, approved novel lists by grade. For information not available online, contact the school district's administrative services center.

Local chambers of commerce are excellent sources of information about major categories of employment in the community, business trends, and economic and workforce development. A chamber's executive director should be one of the library director's key contacts.

NOTES

1. E. Henderson, K. Miller, T. Craig, et al., *Public Libraries Survey: Fiscal Year 2007,* IMLS-2009–PLS-02 (Washington, DC: Institute of Museum and Library Services, 2009), 2.
2. Henderson et al., *Public Libraries Survey.*
3. Ibid.
4. Ibid.
5. Sandra S. Nelson, *Strategic Planning for Libraries* (Chicago: American Library Association, 2008).

CHAPTER TWO

LIBRARY FINANCES

AS ITS VERY name implies, the public library is an entity in the public sector, but although the community may think the library operates like a nonprofit organization, when it comes to finances, it must behave like a government agency. Public libraries are those supported primarily by public funds. These may include funds from the local municipality, township, or county and possibly some locally distributed state and federal monies, and the finances must be managed in accordance with the legal and administrative accounting practices of the governing body. The library director must be fully aware of the main sources of the library's income and the applicable procedures for budgeting, purchasing, accounting, and accountability. State statutes may also specify certain financial practices. For example, the statutes may dictate that the library board has exclusive control of all library expenditures or may prohibit fees for any library service.

WHERE DOES THE MONEY COME FROM?

Most of the funding for U.S. public libraries comes from tax revenue, although the methods of collection and distribution may vary. At the local level, taxes are generally levied on real estate (also known as property taxes), but the local government's funding base may also include revenue from income or sales tax.

LOCAL FUNDING

The library's appropriation may come from a general fund, from a library tax on real estate, or from an earmarked fund. Table 2.1 shows how these different local funding sources work.

TABLE 2.1 : Local funding

Type of funding	Source of funds	How it works	Advantages	Disadvantages
Appropriation from the general fund	Real estate/property taxes (and sometimes income and sales taxes) levied by local government (i.e., city, county, village, township)	All locally funded units (police, fire, parks, libraries, etc.) prepare their annual budgets and present them to the local government executive, budget officer, or finance committee. There may be a hearing for each unit before the final budget is determined.	The local property tax rate can be set to bring in the amount needed. This tax rate is known as millage, with 1 mill equal to $0.01 on each $1,000 of assessed valuation of taxable property.	If the local tax base is shrinking, the library may be competing with other units for its share of the general fund.
Library tax	Usually real estate/property taxes, but levied by a separate library district	The library district board approves the budget.	The board may have the power to raise the taxes to generate the needed amount. The library is not competing for funds with other essential services.	There may be a tax limit that can only be changed by referendum. Appealing directly to voters may require a time-consuming campaign.
Earmarked funds	May come from specific fines or fees or a set percentage of a local sales tax or a tax on a specific industry. The amount may be fixed, so the library budget request is more likely to be based on an estimate of available funds rather than on an assessment of community and program needs.	Earmarked funding has been extremely important in areas of the western U.S., where some counties have a high percentage of federal land that can't be taxed, making it difficult to fund public services through real estate taxes.	The board has more independence and authority. If a number of libraries are funded from one earmarked tax, they may be competing with each other, but they are not competing with other services.	Because the library has not had to build goodwill in the community as part of an annual local budgeting process, the necessary support may not be there when earmarked funding ends.

STATE AND FEDERAL AID

Although very few states provide the primary funding for public libraries in the state budget, it is not unusual for the small public library to receive some state aid either through a direct appropriation or through its membership in a regional library system. *System* is a confusing word because it might refer to a public library and its branches but also, as in this case, to a group of autonomous libraries joined by formal or informal agreements to perform various services cooperatively, such as resource sharing or telecommunications. Systems include multitype library systems and public-library-only systems. The library is usually required to meet certain standards to be eligible for system membership. These standards might include the number of hours that the library is open, the size of the collection budget relative to the population, or a maintenance-of-effort requirement. A maintenance-of-effort policy requires the library's main funding source to maintain a specified level of financial effort.

Library services that are funded with state dollars, whether received directly or indirectly, cover a variety of purposes. In some states, direct grants to libraries have been used to assist communities in building or renovating libraries, to enhance collections, and to upgrade telecommunications capabilities. In other states, funds are used primarily on a statewide basis for services and products such as full-text databases, cooperative cataloging, interlibrary loan and delivery, or collections for people with special needs (such as a library for the blind). In either case the state funds are generally distributed through a state library agency.

Federal funds are rarely a large component of a small public library's budget but can be a helpful supplement to local funding. Most federal funds for libraries are distributed through

Library Closings in Jackson County, Oregon

When the federal government reclaimed land in Oregon in the early twentieth century, the state lost half its property tax base. In exchange, those counties that were heavily impacted received a share of the revenues generated by logging on federal land. These earmarked funds supported excellent schools and libraries, while allowing property tax rates to remain low.

In the 1990s, that system was no longer viable. Logging on federal land had decreased, due partly to environmental regulations and partly to the changing economics of the timber industry. In 2000 Congress passed the Secure Rural Schools and Community Self-Determination Act to continue payments to rural counties for six more years to fund local services. Near the end of that period, a property tax levy was brought to the voters. Passage of the levy would have generated $9 million a year to keep the libraries open, but the voters turned it down. Without a source of funding, Jackson County completely shut down its fifteen libraries in April 2007. The closure of Jackson County's library system was the largest such action in U.S. history. Despite enormous efforts of library supporters, another property tax levy in May 2007 was also defeated.

After Congress passed a one-year extension of the Secure Rural Schools and Community Self-Determination Act, the county decided to outsource the operations of libraries in order to reopen them for at least two and a half years. A private company offered to run the library system for $4.3 million annually, about half the budget before the library closings. How does the company operate the libraries with a much smaller budget? Most of the fifteen libraries in the county are now open about half the hours they were previously. In addition, although the salaries of librarians may be comparable to their salaries in public employment, the level of benefits (such as medical insurance and retirement funds) is generally lower.

the state library agencies. Through the Grants to States program, the Institute of Museum and Library Services provides funds to states using a population-based formula. State library agencies may use the appropriation to support statewide initiatives and services. They also may distribute the funds to local libraries through competitive grants or through cooperative agreements to public, academic, research, school, and special libraries in their state. Each state outlines its programs in a five-year plan that must be approved by the Institute of Museum and Library Services.

Although the amount of state and federal funding may not be large, it is increasingly important because it can fund services that are only cost-effective if done on a large scale. For example, services that cross geographic lines, such as the development of shared resource

---

State Library or State Library Agency?

Not every state has a state library, but every state does have a state library *agency* (which may be called the state library). Though not necessarily actual libraries, these official agencies are charged with statewide library development and with the administration of certain federal funds. The state library agency's functions may or may not include direct library services, archives and records management, library development services, electronic networking and databases, and training/certification of librarians.

All state library agencies provide the following types of services to public libraries:

- administration of Library Services and Technology Act (LSTA) grants
- collection of library statistics
- continuing education programs
- library planning, evaluation, and research
- consulting services
- library legislation preparation or review
- review of technology plans for the E-rate discount

Most state library agencies provide the following:

- administration of state aid
- interlibrary loan referral services
- literacy program support
- reference referral services
- state standards or guidelines
- statewide public relations or library promotion campaigns
- summer reading program support
- union list development

State libraries may offer *direct* services to the following:

- blind persons and individuals with disabilities
- residents of state prisons
- residents of other state institutions
- state archives

When the state agency offers direct library service to the public, it is not in competition with local public libraries but rather for offering services that are fairly specialized and impossible for every library to provide on its own. (Hawaii is an exception, as its state library agency also operates the public libraries throughout the state, which are actually branches of the Hawaii State Public Library System under the jurisdiction of the Hawaii Board of Education.)

systems (and the delivery of materials to the member libraries in such a system), would be difficult to implement fairly if solely dependent on appropriations from each participating local jurisdiction. Therefore librarians not only need to be involved in the local budget process but also should consider becoming involved in the state library association and advisory boards of the state library agency. These groups provide structures for public libraries to develop and present a single voice regarding proposed library legislation and funding and to share opinions regarding the use of federal funds within the state.

ADDITIONAL AND ALTERNATIVE FUNDING

Although taxes are and should be the primary source of funding for public libraries, a significant amount may come from other sources. According to *Public Libraries Survey: Fiscal Year 2007*, 8.7 percent of public library funding came from gifts and donations, grants, interest, library fines, and fees.[1]

Taxpayer "revolts" have often focused on property taxes, the source of most library income. That funding is therefore subject to local politics, the growth or decline of the local tax base, and perhaps the need to solve a budget crisis. Library budgets have often failed to keep up with rising costs for operations, staffing, and new resources and rarely cover the full cost of new buildings or significant expansions or renovations. Federal funds, awarded initially in 1957 through the Library Services Act to fund library service to rural communities, evolved into the Library Services and Construction Act (LSCA), which assisted communities with building projects for over thirty years. However, that act was replaced in 1996 by the Library Services and Technology Act (LSTA), and although this act is an important component of the state and federal funding described earlier, it does not provide funds for construction or for ordinary operating expenses. Many libraries have turned to alternative funding for building projects and for offering additional services.

It is increasingly common to run a capital campaign (for a new building or expansion) outside the normal library budget. However, it is important that library donations, including bequests and financial and volunteer support from the Friends group and any library foundation, be used to enhance publicly funded library services, not to reduce or replace public funding. If the effort of raising supplemental funds does not result in improved service, but instead leads to a reduced government appropriation, it is not an effort worth making.

The librarian in a small community should be familiar with local businesses as well as local service groups such as Rotary and the Jaycees. Service groups may be able to provide financial support, but donations of goods and services from local businesses should also be welcome.

Company-Sponsored or Corporate Foundations versus Corporate Direct Giving Programs: What's the Difference?

Company-sponsored foundations are separate legal entities from the corporation. They must file an annual IRS Form 990-PF. The corporation may make additional gifts to its foundation in profitable years to increase the endowment. Corporate direct giving programs do not have an endowment and do not adhere to private foundation laws or file a Form 990. They enable the corporation to deduct up to 10 percent of its pretax income and may include employee matching gifts.

Items such as additional computer workstations, new furniture, and prizes for summer reading programs present opportunities to acknowledge and publicize the donor as well.

Friends of the Library

A Friends of the Library group offers many benefits to a library. The group may be able to run book sales and other fund-raising activities and use the proceeds to purchase items for the library. (If the library were to run such fund-raising events directly, the revenue might have to be returned to local government coffers.) In addition to fund-raising, a Friends group typically supports the library through volunteer work in the library and through advocacy and "friend-raising." Although the library board and the Friends group share some common goals, they are separate, autonomous bodies, and each has its own distinct role. The Friends' activities should support the library board's plans and policies, and although these volunteers may want a say in how funds are spent, this should be done only after conferring with the library director and board. Book sales are the most common Friends fund-raising activity. In many communities, the library donates books that have been withdrawn from the collection (along with books that have been donated to the library) to the Friends organization for sale to the public. In most jurisdictions the library board has the authority to do this, but because public property is involved, the library board should have a written agreement with the Friends that makes clear that all proceeds from sale of the books (and any other materials) be used to support the programs and services of the library.

A national organization, the Association of Library Trustees, Advocates, Friends and Foundations, exists to motivate and assist state and local library support groups, and its website (http://www.ala.org/ala/mgrps/divs/altaff/index.cfm) offers ideas for fund-raising from groups around the country. Be aware, though, that fund-raising events can be very labor-intensive, so choose events that will truly raise the profile of the library, because the amount of money made may not seem that significant when the hours of labor are added up.

Foundations

Although libraries have long had Friends groups to undertake fund-raising events, some libraries establish foundations to secure major gifts and bequests. Because Friends groups are often

---

TALES FROM THE FIELD: Friends and Funds

Green Lake (Wisconsin) Public Library would not have been the same library without its Friends group. The group holds four book sales a year that fund the entire magazine collection, children's programs, computers, and much more. Members are always looking for new ideas for fund-raising and have done everything from cookie decorating to children's tattoos to a magazine exchange and much more. But their main focus is their book sale, which takes up much of the library's basement on a permanent basis. Dedicated members specially price items throughout the year and work constantly to create a classy, elegant sale.

Source: Tasha Saecker, former director at Green Lake, now assistant director of the Appleton Public Library, Appleton, Wisconsin.

fairly informal, they may never have requested nonprofit status from the Internal Revenue Service—known as IRS 501(c)3 status—and without it, contributions are not tax-deductible. A library foundation, on the other hand, exists solely to raise private money for the support of the library, including capital campaigns for library building projects, and should have tax-exempt status. This 501(c)3 designation also means that the foundation does not pay federal taxes for the income and the interest on that income. Foundations must file IRS Form 990 to report the receipt and expenditure of these funds. Gifts of cash, stocks, real estate, equipment, and other property given to the foundation are tax-deductible for the donor. Some libraries also use a foundation as their recipient for private grant funds, so that grants for special, one-time initiatives are not commingled with public funds for ongoing operating expenses.

Another avenue for tax-deductible contributions when the library does not have its own foundation might be a community foundation. Community foundations are tax-exempt public charities generally dedicated to improving the quality of life in their area. Individuals, families, businesses, and organizations can create permanent charitable funds that can assist organizations in their area while providing tax benefits to the donor. The foundation invests and administers these funds, which may be distributed according to the donor's specifications or according to priorities set by the community foundation's board.

With or without a library foundation, some libraries are now actively soliciting bequests and endowments through what is known as "deferred giving." This type of giving is most likely to be effective when a relationship with a potential donor has been built up over a long period so that a bequest or endowment seems like an appropriate memorial.

Grants

Sometimes a library would like to undertake specific projects that are unlikely to be funded as part of normal operating expenses, such as the digitization of local history materials or the development of a new program area. Such projects may be good candidates for grant funding. Successful project ideas are ones that relate specifically to a library's mission and long-range plan. Private and family foundations are likely to prefer contributing either to capital campaigns for new buildings or to specific projects with measurable outcomes. Grantsmanship is both an art and a skill. It is time-consuming to research potential corporations and foundations, but this investigation is necessary to discover their priorities, their recently funded projects, and their guidelines for submission of requests and proposals. Proposal formats and requirements can vary considerably, and some are extremely complex, but others may involve no more than a letter and budget. Even a small award can have a major impact on a small library's materials or programming budget.

Fines and Fees

Finally, a small portion of the library's budget may come from fines and fees, although in some places fines and fees offset rather than supplement the allocated operating budget. Fines on overdue materials are generally established to provide incentive for the timely return of materials, rather than for the revenue they generate. Some libraries have an annual amnesty or fine-forgiveness day as a way to get back materials that are long overdue. However, some librarians prefer the goodwill and public relations fostered by a no-fines policy, and it is no less effective in getting materials back to the library on time.

Lasting Gifts

Help Your Library Continue to Grow

In 1926, members of the Middleton's Progressive Women's Club decided that Middleton should have a library, which started out with books that each member donated. They placed the books on a single shelf in the dry goods section of the Burmester-Kruse General Store. The population of Middleton then was 900. Now the library has grown into a full-service, 32,000-square-foot facility, a busy community resource that offers diverse resources and services to area residents of all ages: books, magazines, newspapers, audiovisual materials, preschool storytimes, after-school programs, a book discussion group, a computer lab, study rooms, meeting rooms, and more. Middleton's current service-area population has grown to nearly 25,000.

Provide a Lasting Gift to the Library

The Middleton Public Library Endowment Fund was created to encourage private donations and bequests to further the excellence of the library's service program, which is considered one of the best in the nation according to Hennen's American Public Library Ratings. A contribution to the Endowment Fund is a unique opportunity for you to help insure that high-quality library service continues to be a Middleton hallmark.

Choose Your Method of Giving

- A gift of cash, securities, or property for immediate or future use by the library.
- A bequest in your will or living trust to the Middleton Public Library Endowment Fund.
- Beneficiary designations of life insurance or retirement plan proceeds.
- Gifts with retained income for yourself and others.

Unrestricted gifts enable the library to consider its needs and to direct the earnings from these gifts where they are most needed. You may also specify the purpose for which earnings from the gifts are to be used, as long as that purpose and use are consistent with the Library's goals and policies.

Tax Benefits

A gift to the Middleton Public Library Endowment Fund can provide substantial tax savings to the donor, which, in effect, reduces the cost of the gift. Here are some examples.

- Savings in income taxes by gifts of cash, security, or property made during this fiscal year.
- Savings in inheritance and gift taxes, testamentary trusts or gifts, or living trusts.
- Savings in capital gains taxes when gifts of appreciated securities or other property are made.

Be sure to confer with your tax advisor or legal counsel to see whether a gift of this type may be of advantage to you. All contributions to the Endowment Fund are tax-deductible.

I Wish to Provide a Lasting Gift to the Middleton Public Library

My gift is in the amount of ❑ $1,000 ❑ $500 ❑ $100 ❑ $50 ❑ Other _____

In memory / appreciation / on behalf of _____

I would like more information on the following types of gifts:

❑ Securities ❑ Gifts from an estate ❑ Charitable trusts ❑ Real estate ❑ Other _____

Source: Middleton Public Library, Middleton, Wisconsin.

Many state statutes specify that public libraries may not charge "user fees" for public access to library materials. The interests of libraries and their communities are best served when library services are provided without fees of any sort, but there are some exceptions. It is typical to charge patrons for photocopies and computer printouts or to charge for after-hours use of the library's meeting room. Some libraries charge for convenience—for example, having a rental collection of popular DVDs or providing books-by-mail to those who do not wish to come to the library to pick up an interlibrary loan or reserve item (but the library would not charge for delivery to the homebound if that service is provided). In these situations, the materials are also available to patrons at no charge, but without guarantees of when they will be able to borrow them. Keep in mind, though, that it can be difficult to distinguish between a basic service and a special service, and since fees are, in a sense, discriminatory, they should be avoided wherever possible. The cost of collecting fees may outweigh the financial gain.

Another argument against charging fees is that fees represent "double taxation" because library users are already paying for library services through their taxes. But what about services to nonresidents of the community, who are not contributing to the tax base? In some states, state aid is used to compensate libraries for nonresident use. In other areas, library systems may equalize funding to cover borrowing that crosses jurisdictions. The rate of compensation may be determined by reciprocity formulas developed from circulation figures. In the absence of state funding or other cooperative arrangements, a fee may be charged for a nonresident borrower's card. Some libraries charge a minimal fee for the card—perhaps $10—or an amount equivalent to the per capita costs of running the library (in 2005 the national average per capita operating expenditure for public libraries was $31.65), while others charge a larger amount, such as the average annual library tax per household in the area.

TALES FROM THE FIELD: Can You Run a Successful Capital Campaign during an Economic Downturn?

By 2009, the Dwight Foster Public Library in Fort Atkinson, Wisconsin, was running out of room. In 2008, circulation increased 6.5 percent to 197,000 items, and we projected it would top 200,000 items in 2009. Seating space and table space were inadequate. A growing number of people visited the library to use our computers, but people also came with their own laptops and couldn't find a place to sit. We began planning for a $5.5 million, 12,000-square-foot expansion project.

Our library's first expansion was done in 1931, in the midst of the Great Depression. The second expansion dates from 1983, when interest rates were in double digits. In 2009, in spite of the recession, the capital campaign is off to a great start. The city has budgeted $2.5 million, while the Fort Atkinson Community Foundation has pledged $1.5 million. The library needs to raise $1.5 million, and about 70 percent of that has been raised by selling naming rights to parts of the library. A number of fund-raisers aimed at different sectors of the community are planned by the Capital Campaign Committee and the Friends of the Library.

I think it says that when people decide there's a real need, they work together to make it happen. We are a well-used library, and I think that resonates with people and they respond when we ask.

Source: Connie Meyer, Director, Dwight Foster Public Library, Fort Atkinson, Wisconsin.

Sources of Grants

Governmental Grant Programs

- Will have specific program areas
- Will call for proposals at specific times
- Proposal must follow specified format
- Forms and method of submission provided

Examples: Institute of Museum and Library Services, Library Services and Technology Act (administered through state library agencies), National Endowment for the Humanities

To find them:

Grants.gov is a governmental resource to find and apply for federal government grants: www.grants.gov

The Catalog of Federal Domestic Assistance (CFDA) is a database of all federal programs available to state and local governments: https://www.cfda.gov/

Quasi-Governmental Agencies

- May have specific program areas
- May call for proposals at specific times
- Proposal may need to follow specified format

Examples: County development authority, library systems, tribal councils

Foundations

- May have specific program or geographic areas
- May issue Request for Proposal; if not, may require inquiry letters
- Make grants based on charitable endowments

Examples: Private/family foundations, private/independent foundations, community foundations, corporate foundations

To find them:

Foundation finder: http://foundationcenter.org/findfunders/foundfinder/

PREPARING A BUDGET

One of the most serious responsibilities of a library director is the preparation of the budget. A public library should be supported primarily by tax sources, and though supplemental funding from grants, donations, and fund-raising events can help cover the costs of "extras," the budget presented to the library's funding agency must be sufficient to support reasonable levels of staff, materials, utilities, building maintenance, and other necessary costs.

The process starts with gathering information for budget requests. Most budgets will be based on and updated from the previous year's budget, so the last budget year should be reviewed for performance. It is important to consider factors that may be affecting your funding source's overall budget. For example, has there been a change in the tax base in your area or a state-imposed cap on property tax increases? The prevalent inflation rate and the effect of any labor agreements must also be considered. Estimate changes in fixed costs, such as salaries and benefits rate, rent, utilities, and insurance, and price increases for variable costs, such as library materials. Journals such as *Publisher's Weekly* and *Library Journal* report on predicted book prices and periodical and serial increases. Gather external information and input such as census data, surveys or suggestions, and library standards that need to be met. Has there been any change in constituency or any new program requiring support? Are there any new cooperative agreements in place? Is there any equipment that needs repair or replacement? Are there any items that have been held over or deferred from a previous year?

TALES FROM THE FIELD: Library Fees

My library has been renting best sellers for the last two years. Our foundation actually rents or leases the materials from a jobber. Once the title is no longer "hot," the title can be returned to the jobber or purchased at a very discounted price. We just purchase the book and sell it at the book sale. This process has allowed us to provide a service to those that would not normally use the library but use a bookstore. It works very well for the foundation and actually generates revenue. I believe it is a great service for the community and allows free access for those who want to wait for the resource.

—*Steven Nielsen, Director, Bettendorf (Iowa) Public Library*

Public libraries are one of the last bastions of free access to information and attaching a price to this right flies in the face of equality of access. Many libraries charge nominal fees for copying. But to charge fees for the right to access material is something I am vehemently opposed to. Yes, patrons could elect not to pay and wait longer for their turn. But, what this does is relegate the poor to the "back of the bus," due to their inability to "buy" a better seat or place in line. In Policy 61, *Services to the Poor*, the ALA strongly discourages fees for service because it marginalizes the poor.

—*Susan Mannix, Director, LeClaire (Iowa) Public Library*

The library is an equalizer in the sense that the materials are available to all freely and fairly. I think that changing that perception even a little bit may be detrimental. I actually had a call yesterday from a man asking what it cost to get a library card, so we cannot assume that every person understands a library's offerings and services, or get confused about what items are free and which are not.

—*Gloria Drake, Reference Librarian, Oswego, Illinois*

LINE-ITEM BUDGETS

Most municipalities require a line-item budget (see table 2.2). Categories in a line-item budget might include

- salaries
- benefits (sometimes known as fringes)
- materials
- equipment

TABLE 2.2 : Line-item budget

Category	General budget	Detailed budget (examples)
Salaries	All salaries and fringes	• Library director • Children's librarian • Library assistants (position 1, 2, 3, etc.) • Pages • Custodian • Substitutes
Fringe benefits	(included with salary line)	• Fringes @ 35 percent of salaries (may include social security, health and life insurance, retirement plans, unemployment and workers' compensation)
Equipment	All equipment	• Computers • Shelving, book trucks, furniture up to a dollar limit • Leases or maintenance contracts for equipment • Repair/replacement fund for equipment
Supplies and operating expenses	All expenses including materials	• Office, security system, and janitorial supplies • Utilities (telephone, T-1 line, heat, electricity, water/sewer) • Cataloging/processing/electronic records • Printing (PR and program materials) • Postage • Vehicle costs (may be calculated at a per mile rate) • Custodial contract; routine repairs • Insurance • Membership in professional associations • Travel/registration costs for continuing education • Other contracted services
Materials	(included above) Be sure to include any standing orders	• Books (may break down by adult, children's, paperbacks, large print, reference, etc.) • Serial subscriptions (magazines, newspapers) • Audiobooks • Music CDs • DVDs (and possibly videos) • Software/games • License fees for databases • License fees for download services • Other
Capital expenses	May be a separate budget	• New/replacement furniture • New/replacement equipment • Major building repairs or remodeling • New facility costs

- information technology or other contractual services or both
- insurance
- utilities
- supplies
- traveling and training
- capital outlay

How much detail will be needed? The previous year's budget will serve as a template. For example, under salaries and wages, who is included? Is anyone's salary shared with another unit? Does your budget include building security and custodial staff, or is that provided in another department's budget (or included in your rent)? Fringe benefits can include social security (FICA), retirement, medical insurance, life insurance, guaranteed disability income protection, unemployment compensation, workers' compensation, tuition, and housing benefits. Often a predetermined percentage of salary is used. However, that percentage can change from year to year. Operating expenses such as supplies, utilities, insurance, services, and repairs are sometimes consolidated into one category. Capital outlay generally applies to major expenditures over a predetermined sum (such as $5,000). Construction or renovation costs and vehicle or major furniture purchases would fall under a capital budget. Capital budgets are sometimes presented as separate proposals.

If the library's appropriation is from the general fund, the categories of the line-item budget are most likely set up for *all* the various units and functions of local government. However, the library has a major budget category not found in other municipal departments: library materials. Some libraries are allowed to add the collection budget as a category in the line-item budget, but others must fit it into the prevalent budget structure. Although in one sense the collection budget is a capital outlay because it becomes a long-term investment of public dollars (rather than consumable supplies), for purposes of purchasing practices and accountability it is more practical to include the materials budget under operating expenses.

From the standpoint of planning and evaluation, the line-item budget has some drawbacks. It tends to be based on the past and maintains the status quo, with no real review of accomplishments or performance. There is no fiscal evaluation of services and little relationship between the budget request and the objectives of the organization. The budget document reveals little about the functions of a program or department. Its primary value is to provide a way to control what is spent by a department or organization, and perhaps to identify who is accountable for the organization's expenditures.

PROGRAM BUDGETS

Another method of budgeting, called the program budget, bases expenditures on the performance of activities (see table 2.3). Variations of this method include zero-based budgeting and allocation decision accountability performance. The program budget method requires an organization to review and evaluate each of its services and programs on the basis of both outputs and costs. Rather than simply revise a previous year's line-item amount, current activities are reviewed to see if they should be continued—or eliminated or reduced to fund higher-priority new programs or to reduce the current budget. This system is based on a justification for all expenditures of an organization at the time the budget is created. Even if the total library budget is not presented in this way, it is a useful technique for determining the costs of specific activities. (Grant proposal budgets are often developed in this way.) Categories in a program budget might include

- reference services
- service to children and teens
- adult services
- bookmobile
- administration

Each category would include the variable costs of all the activities involved and the fixed costs directly related to the work. The categories might be further divided, showing "summer reading program" under service to children and teens, "homebound delivery" under adult services, and "public relations" under administration. Often a percentage is added for indirect costs or overhead that cannot be easily apportioned to the various program areas. Overhead expenses might include rent, telephone, fax, copying, computer-related expenses, and postage.

An advantage to preparing this type of budget is that it enables government fiscal officers to understand what services they are buying and the cost of each service. This budget type can effectively offer a choice of level of service. If budget cuts must be made, a program budget enables an organization to make these cuts strategically; in other words, rather than just take the same percentage away from all areas of library operations (which may render some services useless or ineffective), the various areas can be evaluated for their cost-benefit value and a decision might be made to eliminate one program rather than weaken all programs. Although small units of government do not typically use an alternative to the line-item budget, library directors should consider preparing a program budget first, with all direct and indirect costs identified, even if it is only used as an internal document. Although it may not be required for

TABLE 2.3 :	Sample program budget for summer reading program	
Resource	**Estimated cost**	**Funded by**
Advertising	$742	Children's Dept. budget
Printing	$497	Local business
Prizes	$950	Local businesses
Performers	3 @ $500 = $1,500	Children's Dept. budget
Refreshments	$400	Local business
Staff time	10 hours per week for 12 weeks @ $17/hour = $2,040	Children's Dept. budget
Staff benefits	35% of salary = $714	Children's Dept. budget
Indirect costs	25% of direct costs = $1,711	Children's Dept. budget
Total	$8,554	

the library's *accounting* system, understanding the actual costs of specific library programs and services will be of great use for *accountability*.

How does one assign dollar amounts to various programs and services provided by the library? Basically the overall line-item budget is subdivided into mini-budgets directly related to the specific areas of library services (see table 2.2). This process does require the accumulation of quantitative data over time—how many staff hours are spent on the reference desk or doing storytime; how many new books must be purchased to have an adequate number for adult book clubs; and so on—and probably a certain amount of informed guesswork. All activities, including those behind the scenes, are prorated among the different services provided by the library. Indirect costs are those not assignable to any one activity and include indirect support services (such as administrative staff time, maintenance, security and custodial services) and indirect operating expenses (such as utilities, rent, telephone, insurance, and equipment).

BUDGET REVIEW

Budget preparation is really a year-round activity, but typically the budget request is put together for presentation to the funding authorities four to six months before the beginning of a new fiscal year. Many governing bodies hold budget hearings in which each unit of government presents its request. The hearing offers a valuable opportunity to explain the library's function, needs, and benefit to the community. The person presenting the budget may be the library director or the board president (with the librarian present to answer questions). What kind of scrutiny can you expect? The amount will vary, but it is critical that the presentation be made by someone who is prepared to provide justification—how certain figures were determined— and can explain succinctly how the budget furthers strategic goals. Brief and clearly written justifications, with meaningful comparisons and statistics, and evidence of citizen support (expressed by written endorsements and the presence and testimony of community leaders) may also be needed when the library is requesting a greatly expanded program.

ACCOUNTABILITY

From time to time the library's financial records will be audited. It is in the public's interest to verify that funds have been spent only for their intended purposes. An audit confirms that all money is accounted for, that accepted accounting procedures have been followed, and that there are no suspicious expenses, which could indicate a conflict of interest or personal gain for someone responsible for the expenditure of public money.

Because libraries receive cash for the payment of fines and for services such as photocopy-ing or computer printing, it is wise to have a cash handling procedure. All amounts received on a daily basis must be recorded and kept secure until the money can be deposited. (If cash inside a photocopier's coin box seems reasonably secure, it can be recorded when the box is emptied.) Deposits should be made weekly. Ideally the components of cash handling—col-lecting, depositing, and reconciling—are separated, so that one individual does not have responsibility for more than one component. In the small library with limited staff it may not

---

TALES FROM THE FIELD: Budget Hearing

I used to do tax preparation so I'm comfortable with numbers and spreadsheets, and I thought doing the library budget would be a snap. Little did I know that the numbers are the least of it! My budget was small and the increases were reasonable but I did not realize how much of the process was tied to presentation and politics. I have learned that I have to be prepared to justify and explain every single line item. And even then, I really want to know ahead of time that I have enough votes on the county board to keep my little budget request intact.

When new members are elected to the county board, I try to meet them well ahead of budget season. I don't want them to think of me as someone who only comes with her hand out! When I show up at a budget hearing, I hope I already know the types of concerns they may have. I try to bring along library board members or patrons who can tell a good story that is related to those concerns.

Sometimes the budget hearing seems to pit us against other worthwhile services. One time the library budget was on the schedule right after the fire department budget and then an item regarding financing for services for the disabled, and the meeting room was filled with volunteer firefighters and people in wheelchairs. The finance committee chair said to me, "Well, tell us why the library is more important than fire protection or helping the disabled." I answered, "I don't envy you the job of deciding if A is *more* important than B, but that is *your* job—my job is to tell you why the *library* is important, not to suggest that other things are not. And I'd like to introduce some members of our community who want to tell you why the library is important to them."

Source: Submitted by an Indiana librarian.

---

be possible to separate these activities, so someone not directly involved with the cash receipt process such as a board member or government fiscal officer should have the responsibility to reconcile monthly cash activity and compare actual deposits recorded with expected receipts.

Accountability also includes keeping your records in a manner consistent with the public library annual report data that your state library agency collects. Along with figures for library services and programs (such as circulation statistics or attendance at children's programs), consistent financial reporting makes it possible to compare public libraries and relate the value received to the price paid. Categories for annual report data may include

Revenue from

- municipal appropriation
- county appropriation
- library district appropriation
- state funds
- federal funds
- contract income
- all other income
- total income

Expenditures for

- salaries and wages
- employee benefits

- print materials
- electronic format
- audiovisual materials
- all other materials
- library materials total
- contracted services
- other operating expenditures
- total operating expenditures
- capital outlay
- tax rates/support per capita

Accountability, though, goes beyond the administrative and accounting rules that must be followed. The *appearance* of a conflict of interest or a personal gain for a staff or board member, even when there has been no violation, can be just as damaging as an actual conflict of interest or personal gain. When in doubt about the propriety of a financial action, have as many people as possible involved in the decision, and ask the board to put its decision on record.

TERMINOLOGY

These terms are integral to the financial management of a library:

Appropriation. An authorized or estimated expenditure level—the budget for a line item.

Line item. An account such as supplies, salaries, or books.

Cash basis accounting. Receipts are recognized when received in cash, rather than when earned, and expenses are recognized when payment is made, rather than when the liability is incurred.

Accrual basis accounting. Income is reported when earned/allocated, and expenses are reported when incurred.

Encumbrance. A commitment that is not yet a liability; money set aside to pay for an obligation or to purchase goods or services.

Fund. Separate accounting and reporting entities that are used to segregate specific activities. The primary operating fund is usually known as the General Fund.

Purchase order. A tool used to encumber funds for a liability and to issue an order for the purchase to take place; also used for certification of the availability of funds.

NOTE
1. E. Henderson, K. Miller, T. Craig, et al., *Public Libraries Survey: Fiscal Year 2007*, IMLS-2009–PLS-02 (Washington, DC: Institute of Museum and Library Services, 2009).

CHAPTER THREE

PERSONNEL MANAGEMENT

THE LARGEST PORTION of almost any library's budget is allocated to salaries and related benefits for library personnel. Just as books and other library materials are carefully chosen and organized to make best use of a limited budget, so too should the library's human resources be carefully selected and nurtured. There are basic principles and practices that may be familiar to you if you have had responsibility for human resources in almost any line of work. The areas of recruiting, hiring, and supervising staff are found in most types of employment. Some aspects of personnel management apply to volunteer staff as well.

Personnel issues are often the first "management test" of a new library director. Although one would take some time to become familiar with the organization and community before embarking on, say, a strategic plan or the annual budget, the new director may be faced straightaway with a vacant position, a disgruntled employee, a workplace injury, or other staffing situation that requires immediate attention. Although the board has the responsibility of hiring and evaluating the director, the director is generally responsible for all other staff.

Every library can take some simple steps to ensure that staff members present the library in a positive light and are able to respond to a variety of situations, including emergencies. If you are a newly hired director, gather the information all staff members should know and include it in all staff training. Such knowledge will not only demonstrate to patrons that the library is run in a professional way but also help staff members feel more comfortable and competent. Sometimes even staff members who have been employed for a while will not be familiar with all this information, and the arrival of a new director (or any other new hire) is a good excuse to provide a "refresher orientation" for all.

What All Staff Members Need to Know

All staff should know

- What to do in an emergency; location of phone numbers for emergency services (see checklist in chapter 4)
- Where the fire extinguishers are and how to use them
- When and how to evacuate the building
- What to do in a severe weather emergency (tornado, flood, etc.)
- What to do if someone is stuck in the elevator (if the library has one)
- How to answer the most basic questions: location of bathrooms and meeting rooms, library hours, how to get a library card

Everyone at the circulation or reference desk should be able to quickly locate

- An up-to-date copy of the library's policies
- A copy of the library's current budget
- The names of the library board members and information on board meeting times
- Information about the library's Friends group, if you have one

Everyone at the circulation or reference desk should know

- When the library was built
- Where today's programs and meetings in the library are being held
- The library's policies on borrowing periods, renewals, and fines
- The URL of the library's website, and the library's and/or library director's e-mail address
- How to handle complaints about library materials
- How to handle requests for information by law enforcement officials
- How to provide patrons with the names of elected officials
- What tax forms are available at the library
- How patrons can apply for any special services (homebound delivery, Talking Books, etc.)

The library director should know

- The names of all library board members
- The names of the main elected officials in the library's service area (mayor, county executive, town chairman, school board, etc.) and have a file with contact information for each one
- The size of the library budget (and at least a rough estimate of the amounts in major categories)
- How to explain how library money is spent

PERSONNEL POLICIES

Various federal, state, and sometimes local laws and regulations impact the selection of employees and their treatment in the workplace. Many of these laws are designed to protect employees. Personnel policies often address the legal issues and, in specifying the library's procedures regarding hiring, compensation, working conditions, and the like, demonstrate compliance with these laws. Even libraries with a single staff member, hourly wages, and no fringe benefits should have a written policy to describe, for example, provision for a substitute librarian, or whether time off with pay is given for any reason (such as jury duty or funeral leave). As with other policies, the library director can and should recommend personnel policy changes but can implement only those policies officially approved by the board.

Certain points should be present in all personnel policies, while others may be specific to the work setting. Some areas may be covered in the personnel policy that apply to all employees of your local government, such as eligibility for benefits, types of leave allowed, disciplinary policy, and grievance procedures. Between any such larger personnel policy and a policy or employee handbook written specifically for the library, the following points should be addressed:

- hiring procedures
- work schedule
- compensation
- payroll information and timekeeping procedures
- benefits
- workers' compensation information and procedures
- performance assessment procedures

All library employees should have job descriptions that list the essential duties of each position, any education and experience required, the physical and mental requirements of the job, and the salary range. These elements should be reviewed and updated regularly, and it is particularly important to do so before filling a vacant position or adding a new position. Job responsibilities tend to change over time for two reasons. First, the organization's needs may change, or new technologies or organizational structures may make certain duties obsolete. For example, participation in a shared resource system may mean that pages not only shelve materials but also pull items for delivery to other libraries. The need for basic computer instruction for patrons may diminish as fewer arrive without *any* computer skills, but requests for more complex instruction in the use of databases may increase. A school district's addition of kindergarten for four-year-olds may result in fewer in-library storytimes and more outreach to schools.

The second factor in changing job responsibilities comes from the incumbents, particularly those who cover a variety of roles and function fairly independently. Over time, there is a tendency—conscious or unconscious—to spend more time on the parts of the job that provide the most satisfaction. This is not necessarily a bad thing. The staff member who discovers an aptitude for writing successful grant proposals or making puppets or designing eye-catching posters or leading adult book discussions may enlarge that part of the job, and the library is all the richer for it. However, when that position becomes vacant, it is a good time to examine the library's needs and craft a position description that will start the next person off in the direction that is most needed.

Job descriptions and requirements should comply with the Americans with Disabilities Act (ADA; www.ada.gov), the federal Fair Labor Standards Act, and any state statutes regarding fair employment practices. The ADA requires reasonable accommodations in three areas of employment—in the application process, in the work environment, and in access to benefits. Job descriptions should be written so that the essential functions—the fundamental requirements

Sample Personnel Policy

Authority

- The library board shall select, appoint, and when necessary for valid reasons, dismiss the director of the library.
- The board shall establish all other positions and all wage and benefit levels for all library staff.
- The library board shall conduct annual appraisals of the library director's performance, at which time personal and management goals can be discussed and negotiated.
- The director will be responsible for preparing annual performance assessments for library staff and volunteers.

Salaries

A classification and salary schedule has been adopted by the library board. The plan is subject to regular revision so that it will remain equitable for both the library and the staff. Salaries are based on the levels of responsibility, experience, and education required of the position for which they have been established.

Health Insurance Policy

The director and any other full-time employees shall receive, as part of the compensation package, health insurance benefits equal to those offered other employees of the municipality. The employee level of contribution to the health insurance plan is subject to change annually.

Vacation Policy

Full-time employees accrue a paid vacation entitlement of 15 work days (120 hours) per fiscal year of full-time employment. Employees with an appointment between 50 percent time and full-time accrue vacation based on their percentage of appointment. In determining vacation schedules, the supervisor shall try to accommodate the employee's wishes, subject to workload demands on the library. Employees are encouraged to use vacation in the year in which it accrues, but may carry over up to 60 hours for no longer than one year.

Holiday Policy

Full-time employees are granted nine days of paid legal holidays per calendar year. Employees must be in pay status either the first work day prior to the holiday or the first work day following the holiday to be eligible to receive the paid holiday. Part-time employees are paid for legal holidays, prorated to the percentage of their employment.

Sick Leave

Full-time employees earn eight hours of sick leave per month, which may be accumulated. Part-time employees receive up to four days of non-accumulating personal leave per year, prorated to the percentage of their employment.

Leave of Absence

Leaves of absence without pay may be granted to library employees for maternity, adoption, illness, bereavement, travel, or graduate, certification, or military training. All leaves are considered on a case-by-case basis and must be approved by the director. A leave for the director must be approved by the library board.

With the exception of bereavement leave or military orders, requests for leave should be submitted in writing well in advance of the time when the leave is to begin. Written requests should indicate both a beginning and ending date for the leave. Vacation time must be used before an unpaid leave will be approved for reasons other than maternity, adoption, or military training. When an employee is on unpaid leave he or she is responsible for all health insurance costs and other benefit premiums/deductions that may apply.

Jury Duty

In the event a library employee is called for jury duty, the library will release him or her and assure no loss of wages. If fees and expenses paid to jurors do not equal or exceed wages normally paid by the library, these fees can be turned in to the library board and the employee will be paid his or her wages as usual.

Work Schedule Policy

Major changes in the director's schedule or other circumstances may not be made without approval of the library board. Requests for such shall be made in writing to the library board. Requests for changes in the work schedule of other staff or volunteers shall be made in writing to the library director.

Professional Development

The director, staff, and trustees attending continuing education opportunities to aid the library shall be allowed expenses at the discretion of the library board according to the amount appropriated in the budget for such. The director, staff, and trustees are encouraged to attend and participate in continuing education activities.

Disciplinary Policy

An employee of the library may be dismissed for any action or behavior that causes the library's image or operation to be diminished. This includes but is not limited to: incompetence, misconduct, inattention to assigned duties, or unapproved absences from work.

Disciplinary steps include

1. A substandard performance appraisal

2. Verbal and/or written warnings

3. Suspension, and/or extended probation

4. Termination

While notice of intent to terminate can be expected, the library reserves the right to dismiss an employee without notice in cases involving theft, drug or alcohol abuse, criminal activity, or significant misconduct.

Resignation and Retirement Policy

A library employee wishing to resign or retire from employment must notify the director or the library board as soon as practicable. The library requests a minimum notice of two weeks. For the library director a notice of at least one month is preferred. The employee must submit a formal, written resignation statement giving the exact date that employment is to be terminated. If the employee is entitled to benefits (such as earned, unused vacation), a lump sum payment can be made to the employee.

Grievance Procedure

Every employee shall have the opportunity to express concerns relating to the physical surroundings in which the employee works, procedures and conditions of the specific position, relationships with fellow workers or supervisors, and library rules as they apply to staff. A concern or grievance should follow the procedure below:

1. If possible, discuss the problem with the director. In the case of the director having a concern, this should be discussed with the board president.

2. If the director is part of the problem, or if the board president is part of the director's problem, the concern/grievance should be submitted in writing for the library board and be delivered to the director, who will deliver the statement to the board president. The board president will, in turn, present the concern, during closed session, to the full board at the next or a special board meeting.

3. The board's representative will respond to the employee within five (5) days of the board meeting at which the issue is discussed, providing either a determination, a solution, or a strategy for how the board will address the issue over time.

Equal Employment Opportunity Policy

It is the policy of the library to provide an equal employment opportunity for all qualified and qualifiable persons. Equal employment opportunity shall be according to the provisions of state and federal laws and regulations.

of a position—are clear. Although reasonable accommodations must be made to allow a qualified person with a disability to do the work, those essential functions need not be modified. If marginal aspects of the position might exclude persons with disabilities, consider whether another staff member could take on those tasks. For example, if a job description requires that an employee be able to lift fifty pounds, that requirement may be essential if loading boxes of books onto the system delivery truck is a daily event, but it is marginal if the employee might need to move something once a month and could ask someone else to do it. Reasonable accommodation for various disabilities might include modifying a workstation, offering adjustable chairs and adaptive equipment, or possibly restructuring the job schedule. It is worth remembering that reasonable accommodation does not only apply to new hires. Any of us could require some type of accommodation at any time in order to continue productive work lives.

In recognizing the need for new roles and for defining a new job, first look at whether any of the work should or can be done by existing staff. Someone may be hoping for the opportunity to expand into a new area, and that possibility may affect what goes into the new job description for the vacant position. After a job description has been drafted, estimate the salary range for the position. It should be consistent with the existing structure and the salary of other employees at that level. In some situations, feedback and authorization from the board or municipal human resources office may be required.

HIRING

A personnel policy may not provide details of all hiring procedures, but the steps should be documented in a procedures handbook. For example, the library should be consistent in addressing the following questions:

- Where are vacant positions posted or advertised?
- Is there a minimum amount of time that job announcements must appear?
- Do you want to give current employees first shot at the job?
- Who screens the applications? Who conducts interviews?
- What is the practice regarding checking references?
- Are background checks required?
- When offering a position, is a verbal offer followed by a written offer that specifies salary, benefits, supervisor, probationary period, or other details?
- Is there a checklist for orientation of new employees?

What if no suitable candidate applies for a position that has been advertised? Consider whether the job requirements are too stringent for the pay grade or are an odd mix. Here's an example:

> Our library is in need of an innovative individual with an interest in marketing and graphic design to serve as a part-time Library Assistant II (25 hours per week). Duties include adult programming, graphic design, marketing, and circulation. The individual will be responsible for designing web pages, posters, and brochures, and creating catchy Twitter and Facebook posts. Hours are

primarily evenings and every third Saturday. A college degree and additional course work in Library and Information Science or work experience in a public library are required. Desirable skills include: familiarity with different printing processes and applications such as Adobe Photoshop, Adobe Illustrator, Adobe InDesign, Macromedia Dreamweaver, Adobe Bridge. Fluency in Spanish preferred. $14.11 per hour to start.

Conducting an Interview

Have extra copies of the job description at the interview.

Describe the job and the organization, but don't talk too much (you want to see if the applicant has made the effort find out about the organization).

Ask the same questions of all candidates.

Ask about compensation/benefit needs and expectations.

If the interview is being conducted by a committee, have a member of the committee take notes. Have all interviewers share their impressions right after the interview.

Ask challenging, open-ended questions:

   What skills do you bring to the job?

   What concerns do you have about filling this role?

   What was your biggest challenge in a past job, and how did you meet it?

   How do you get cooperation on a project from people who don't actually report to you?

Of course, the length of the interview and the type of questions are related to the level of the position and the amount of initiative expected from a successful candidate. But even teenagers who are interviewing for page positions can be asked questions that allow them to demonstrate their maturity and reliability (rather than just asking "What hours can you work?").

Don't ask about personal information (although you can answer questions related to personal information if it has been brought up by the candidate):

   Are you married?

   Do you have children?

   Are you planning to have children?

   Is your husband/wife a student?

   Will you be moving when he or she graduates?

   Wow, you finished college ten years before I was born! Aren't you thinking about retiring?

Discuss relevant personnel policies such as probationary periods.

Let the applicant know your time line for filling the position, and get back to her or him in a timely fashion.

Ask for references. Check the references!

Is it realistic to expect that one person will have this combination of skills and education (and also be willing to take a support staff position at this pay rate)? It might be necessary to rewrite the job description so that the required skills and training are somewhat similar to other library assistant positions, or to upgrade the job level. Another possibility would be to hire someone who has strength in one of the areas described and plan for dedicated training to bring her or his other skills to the needed levels.

PERSONNEL RECORDS

What should you keep in an employee's personnel file? Although few of us enjoy dealing with paperwork, the time spent maintaining personnel records will be far less than the time needed to re-create events and documents should they be needed. A basic file for each employee should contain the job description for the position, the job application or resume or both, the offer of employment, the date of hire, and the IRS Form W-4 (the Employee's Withholding Allowance Certificate). You will also want to file forms relating to employee benefits and forms providing next of kin and emergency contacts.

If employees are initially hired with probationary status, after that period the file should be updated with the initial evaluation, if a formal one was done. Performance evaluations, awards, completion of training programs, raises, and promotions should be included in the file.

All employees complete an I-9 form from the U.S. Citizenship and Immigration Services (USCIS; formerly the U.S. Immigration and Naturalization Service) to verify that the employees are legally authorized to work in the United States. Rather than filing this form with each individual's personnel record, all the forms should be stored together in one folder, because the USCIS is entitled to inspect these forms. If such an inspection does occur, it will not compromise the privacy of employees.

If you ever have to fire a problem employee, the documentation found in a well-kept personnel record will support the action taken and protect the library in the event of a lawsuit. Such documentation might include performance evaluations; dated, written warnings or notices of disciplinary actions; and notes on attendance and tardiness, if these are problems.

WORK SCHEDULES

The standard workweek often does not apply in libraries, as employees must be scheduled to cover evening and weekend hours, and many may have part-time appointments. However, clear expectations for workday hours are still essential, particularly for those who may be responsible for opening or closing the building. Staff should have a clear understanding of timekeeping procedures, the time allowed for lunch/dinner breaks and other break times, and who to call if an absence is unavoidable due to illness, severe weather, or other emergency.

Normally, any other time off, such as vacation or personal days, should be requested in advance. Regarding time off that extends beyond an employee's earned vacation time, a personnel policy may set rules for leaves of absence, including military leave, funeral leave, maternity leave, or jury duty.

COMPENSATION

All employees should be informed about basic compensation matters: the dates of pay periods; regulations regarding payment of overtime or compensation time, or both; salary ranges and salary review policy; and the requirements for promotional increases, if applicable. At the time of hire, and whenever there are changes that affect net compensation, clear communication is crucial. Required and voluntary payroll deductions, changes in benefits or co-pay amounts,

---

TALES FROM THE FIELD: Circulation Desk Staffing

The County Public Library is a small but busy library that is open sixty-four hours a week, seven days a week. The circulation desk staff consists of a full-time circulation manager and eight part-time clerks. There is a fair amount of employee turnover in the circulation department. The library has had problems finding and hiring staff. The library wages are low. None of the desk staff had library training when hired. Lucy has worked at the library for eight years, which is longer than the other clerks. The other clerks have worked at the library at least two years. The hours worked by the clerks range from ten hours to twenty-four hours per week.

For the past year, clerks' availabilities to work have become an issue. Three clerks have limited availability for working at the library: Joan and Jack are students, and Lisa works a different job during the day. Since school started in the fall, there have been times that the circulation desk has not been adequately staffed and desk tasks have not been done. For security reasons and for customer service reasons, the desk is supposed to be staffed by three clerks, but frequently there are only two available. There is no one to call in to replace a sick clerk.

Recently, the staffing situation has gotten worse because some clerks have reduced their availability even more. Rose and Lois both decided to go to school, in order to work in the health care field. Rose only wants to work eight hours a week, and recently said she wants to work at the library so that she can talk to adults. Lois is unavailable two days a week, and does not want to work evenings or weekends. Helen only wants to work eight hours a week only after 5 p.m., does not like working weekends, and is usually late for work. Helen has also applied for non-library jobs.

The circulation manager has started complaining to the director about how time-consuming and difficult it is to schedule enough staff at the desk because of the limited availability of certain desk clerks. She also mentions that she has received complaints about Helen and Lisa from customers— and from other staff. Lisa has admitted herself that she has difficulty remembering how to do desk tasks. Though the circulation manager means to address these performance issues, she's not terribly comfortable with this aspect of the supervisor's role, and the limited working hours of these two clerks makes it easy for her to avoid the issue.

In order to get depth back into circulation staffing, the director, in consultation with the board and the county human resources officer, would like to hire two or three new clerks who will work twenty to thirty hours per week, while letting two or three of the present staff go. (The budget will not allow for keeping all existing clerks and new clerks.) The human resources officer has raised the following questions:

Why is the pool of potential employees poor or inconsistent? Where could the library look for employees that would be better fits for the library?

How will the rest of the library staff react if two or three clerks were let go? How will the new hires be received? How will the circulation manager and director manage the changes?

Source: Gisela Newbegin, DeForest (Wisconsin) Area Public Library.

library closures for severe weather or furloughs, or even a change in pay periods can impact take-home pay and cause financial stress, particularly at the lower end of the pay scale.

It can be a challenge for a small community to adequately fund library positions. For many workers job satisfaction does not rest solely on compensation, but focuses on meaningful work and the opportunity to "make a difference." That intrinsic satisfaction does not mean that a library administrator and board should not strive to offer competitive salaries (you don't want to lose a skilled staff member to the local supermarket when it turns out that she can make twice as much checking groceries as checking out books), but it does mean that salary is not the only factor in creating a pleasant work environment. Providing sufficient training so everyone feels competent, and looking for opportunities for growth and staff recognition are equally important to the successful recruitment and retention of staff.

At the same time, it is useful to gather salary data about employees doing comparable work in local government offices and school districts. If library employees are not receiving comparable salaries, this discrepancy should be brought up in the library budget cycle. If low wages are resulting in high staff turnover and customer service problems, this too should be documented.

BENEFITS

Clear, written information should be available regarding the benefits offered with each position, including eligibility and general information, types of available benefits, and costs (if any) to the employee. Often, only full-time employees are eligible for the complete range of benefits. Part-time employees may receive a prorated share of benefits or may receive no benefits at all (particularly those working fewer than twenty hours per week).

Benefits fall into three main categories. The first benefit category is paid time off (PTO). Some organizations divide this category into separate allotments for vacation, personal days, sick leave, and paid holidays; others group everything but holidays into a general PTO allotment. The amount of paid time off that can be carried over from one fiscal (or calendar) year to the next should be clearly stated.

The second category of benefits is the most significant financially—both as part of the employee's compensation package and in the library's budget. These benefits include social security contributions, medical insurance, dental insurance, disability or income continuation insurance, group life insurance, and pension or other retirement plan. Employees are often required to pay a portion of insurance premiums. Eligibility for various benefits and any required employee contributions should be provided in writing when offering a position.

The third category of benefits includes those that may be offered for employees to use as needed. These might include access to employee advisory/assistance resources, such as smoking cessation programs or financial counseling, or continuing education resources, such as tuition reimbursement for those working toward a degree or travel and registration fees for conferences or professional development workshops. Some employers offer employee reimbursement accounts, which allow employees to set aside pre-tax income for eligible medical or dependent care expenses, or both.

Finally, all workplaces should have readily available information on workers' compensation procedures and benefits—what to do when an injury or accident occurs on the job, and what types of injuries and expenses are covered under workers' compensation.

SUPERVISION

The supervisory role means different things to different managers. Some hope that it means no more than scheduling staff and making work assignments. If a staff member is underperforming or a conflict arises between coworkers, these managers assume that in time, staff turnover will solve the problem. If they are required to do performance evaluations, they tend to rely on forms, giving most employees the same slightly above-average rating and filing the evaluations (or submitting them to a human resources office) without discussing them with the staff.

Of course, many new library directors have supervisory experience in other settings and have learned through that experience that supervision also includes encouraging and developing positive staff relationships and helping staff members find intrinsic motivation for good performance. These supervisors communicate their goals for the library and explain how *every* position in the library helps to contribute to those goals. Such directors serve as coaches rather than scorekeepers when someone is underperforming.

There is a considerable body of management literature[1] devoted to this leadership aspect of personnel management—at an individual level as a mentor or coach, at a group level to build teamwork and resolve conflicts, and at an institutional level to build organizational culture. One of the tools at a group as well as individual level is the performance appraisal—not the typical annual ranking form that is usually the basis for determining the employee's pay increase, but a performance discussion that provides meaningful feedback to employees, helps them set goals for self-development, and acknowledges the employees' own hopes for extrinsic and intrinsic rewards.

Performance-related discussions do not require a formal, full-scale performance appraisal/ rating system. Such coaching sessions can shape and improve employee performance before undesirable patterns have set in. Although good performance should be regularly acknowledged, it's also nice to set aside a time to go through an employee's job description, praise what has been done well, and ask what help the individual needs to do a better job in other areas. In a small library, the supervisor may have firsthand knowledge of each person's performance, but if interaction with some employees is limited because of shifts that don't overlap, the supervisor should consult others to appreciate fully how employees contribute. If some parts of a job description have been seriously neglected, it might be because that task is regularly done by someone else or is no longer needed. Often the person in the position is the best one to suggest modifications to the job description.

By identifying the types of rewards that motivate each individual, it may be possible to help him or her identify new challenges and find opportunities to grow on the job. The appropriate reward system can reduce absences and attrition, increase employee satisfaction and commitment to the organization, and even influence someone's long-range occupational and organizational choice.

Motivating Others

Getting the best from others is usually a matter of understanding what they care about and what they need—then doing all you can to align that with the requirements of the job and the organization.

Extrinsic motivators—pay, job security, promotion, working conditions—are effective at keeping people on the job, but won't necessarily bring out everyone's best work. Intrinsic motivation comes from interest in one's job, feelings of accomplishment, and the sense of shared responsibility for larger goals. Managers who do not want or know how to share responsibility may find that they have become either too passive, assuming minimal responsibility for the success of a project or organization, or too controlling, taking personal responsibility—and credit—for success. Either way, this type of manager avoids the kind of supervision that gets the best from staff, perhaps from fear of not getting the hoped-for response from others, and may come to believe the adage, *"If I want something done right, I have to do it myself."* In the terms of the following table, that manager is operating in a controlling frame, while the manager who seeks to share responsibility is operating in a cooperative way.

	Controlling manager	**Cooperating manager**
Self	I'm the one who knows how this should be done.	I have information and experience, but may not understand or think of everything.
Staff member	Uninformed, or even incompetent or ill-intentioned	May see things that I don't see which could contribute to my understanding
Task	Make them see: *My way or the highway!*	Access our collective knowledge and experience in order to make the best choice

Note: Quotation and table adapted from Melanie Hawks, *Focus On: Motivating Others* (Washington, DC: ARL Office of Leadership and Management Services, 2005). This tip sheet is one in a series entitled Focus On: Leading Library Transformation, from the Association of Research Libraries (ARL) Office of Leadership and Management Services, ©ARL/OLMS 2005.

The rating type of performance evaluation may still be required to determine the employee's pay increase or eligibility for promotion. The results of this kind of appraisal are not usually much of an incentive, because in the public sector it often amounts to no more than a cost-of-living increase, and differences between the maximum and minimum increases are often quite modest. Those doing the ratings also have a tendency to rank toward the middle. If the money available for raises is limited, not everyone can get a high rating. If increases are allocated as percentages, employees in higher pay ranges receive greater rewards even if work is inferior.

DISCIPLINE AND GRIEVANCES

What if you have inherited staff members with some problematic work behaviors and find that they have always received above-average performance ratings? For example,

The employee who is often five to ten minutes late for her work (but records on her time card that she arrived on time)

The teenage pages (in their first paying jobs) who forget that they aren't there to just hang out and talk to their friends who come in after school

The long-term employee who is decidedly unhelpful and sometimes just plain rude to patrons

Although staff members who are struggling with certain tasks or skills on the job may be helped with patient training, attitude problems are much harder to deal with—and, as a result, may have been left unchallenged. When the positive approach to improving an employee's performance does not work, more formal action may be needed. Disciplinary action is the action taken by an organization against an employee for performing below a certain level or violating an institutional rule. Performance problems or violations should be documented in writing. Any warnings or other disciplinary actions should be noted in the employee's personnel file, as should notes on attendance and tardiness, if these are problems. No matter how many times the problem has occurred, if it has not been addressed before, it should be treated as a first infraction, with a warning given. The personnel policy should include a written plan that identifies consequences for subsequent problems, which might include a temporary reduction in hours, followed by suspension and ultimately dismissal. The disciplinary action might also include a plan for specific behavior changes that the employee must agree to.

Complaints from patrons or coworkers should be treated carefully. If you cannot personally verify the incident that prompted a complaint, consider the credibility of the complaint and make a point of observing the employee over time. On one hand, if the complaint is a result of a misunderstanding or a demanding patron's personality or is out of character for the employee, a note in a personnel file could unfairly damage someone's reputation. On the other hand, if such complaints are never written up (for just this reason), this omission could result in a long pattern of poor customer service or an uncomfortable setting for other employees, without the documentation to do anything about it.

A grievance is any dissatisfaction relating to one's employment that is brought to the attention of an organization's management. Employees may have complaints about the director, about other employees, or about library policy or operations. Many managers have an open-door policy and encourage employees to bring such concerns to them before they become full-fledged grievances. Even when the complaint concerns the director, the board should direct employees to bring up the situation with their supervisor or the director. Staff complaints should go directly to the board only when there is no other avenue available.

In a unionized library, the collective bargaining agreement most likely outlines a formal process for employee grievances. This process involves the reporting of problems through the union and provides representation for the aggrieved employee, but it is limited to contractual issues.

TALES FROM THE FIELD: Boosting Staff Morale

I believe that making each staff member feel like a vital part of the team that makes the library succeed is key to staff morale. Staff members need to know that they are valued (small positive comments on at least a daily basis), that the work they are doing is important (while staff members know how the entire system works, each has a "specialty" for which he or she holds primary responsibility), and that all are held in respect for themselves and their work as well as held accountable for their individual work.

Perhaps modeling good attitude and ability to "roll with the punches" when a bad day or bad situation occurs is the best morale booster. When your staff know that you aren't going to lose your temper or fall into a blue funk, but adopt a positive attitude and maintain an even keel through adversity, their morale is boosted. That, coupled with fair (please note the difference between "fair" and "equal") treatment for staff and patrons alike, and equal opportunity for training, advancement, and even voicing opinions (on collection, circulation, personnel matters, etc.) for all the staff, fosters good morale. Instituting an "open-door" policy, where staff know they can come and discuss issues with you in private and in confidence, as well as in staff meetings when appropriate, is another key to good morale.

Source: Ann Ammerman, Director, Suring (Wisconsin) Public Library.

At times the library board may become involved in personnel issues. Board meetings are typically subject to a state's open meeting regulations. However, there are times when a board is allowed to meet in closed session to discuss personnel issues. These might include the annual review of the library director, a discussion of the compensation to be offered to a specific job candidate, disciplinary actions, and grievances that cannot be resolved by the director. State statutes regarding open meetings generally list the allowable exceptions.

VOLUNTEERS

A volunteer is a person who performs tasks for the library without wages, benefits, or other compensation. Although it can be challenging for a small library with a small budget to adequately staff all areas of library service, volunteers should provide a supplement to the efforts of paid library staff, not a replacement for them. Keep in mind that effective use of volunteers also requires staff time for recruiting, training, and finding appropriate projects.

In recruiting volunteers, it is especially important to think about intrinsic motivators. Volunteer talents, experience, and interests should be considered. People who volunteer do so for various reasons:

- for the personal satisfaction of performing a service that is valued by the community
- to share a skill or area of expertise
- to get job experience
- to satisfy service learning requirements in school
- to meet people

The library should have policies regarding volunteers, such as minimum age and guidelines for conduct. Job descriptions should be written for any volunteer positions that are filled on a regular basis (as opposed to one-time volunteers at special events). If the work requires training by library staff, a minimum time commitment may be needed.

The library should provide appropriate recognition of volunteers' services. This acknowledgment could be a reception honoring volunteer service, a press release to the local paper, a listing of volunteer names in the annual report, a certificate of appreciation, or the addition of a book to the collection in each volunteer's name.

NOTE

1. Joan Giesecke and Beth McNeil, *Fundamentals of Library Supervision* (Chicago: American Library Association, 2005); James M. Kouzes and Barry Z. Posner, *The Leadership Challenge*, 4th edition (San Francisco: Jossey-Bass, 2007); and Peter R. Scholtes, Brian L. Joiner, and Barbara J. Streibel, *The Team Handbook*, 3rd edition (Madison, WI: Oriel, 2003).

CHAPTER FOUR

FACILITIES

DEFINING LIBRARY SPACES

Since the mid-1980s, a series of planning documents and other publications have advanced the concept of the public library as a central and essential part of its community.

The library as a community center. "The library is a central focus point for community activities, meetings, and services"—one of the eight public library service roles described in *Planning and Role Setting for Public Libraries: A Manual of Options and Procedures* (American Library Association, 1987).

The library as commons. "The library helps address the need for people to meet and interact with others in their community and to participate in public discourse about community issues"—one of thirteen public library service responses enumerated in *Planning for Results: A Public Library Transformation Process* (American Library Association, 1998).

The Library as Place: History, Community, Culture. This 2007 Libraries Unlimited publication, edited by John Buschman and Gloria J. Leckie, contains fourteen essays that describe the library as a physical, social, and intellectual space.

"Libraries at the Heart of Our Communities." In the summer 2009 issue of the *Planning Commissioners Journal*, publisher and editor Wayne Senville touts libraries as "economic engines" of downtown and neighborhood development.

All these examples promote libraries as vital, active, and essential parts of their communities. To participate fully in this role, however, library staff and board members are well advised to take an inventory of how their library is positioned in the community, both physically and virtually.

THE VIRTUAL LIBRARY

A library's virtual presence often provides area residents, particularly newcomers to a community, with their first glimpse of what the library has to offer. For this reason, a library's website should establish a virtual presence that is as strong and unambiguous as its physical one. At a minimum, the following information should be found, if not on a library's home page, no more than one click away. And when links are used, they should always be prominently displayed.

- location and general contact information (official name of library, street address, telephone/fax numbers, e-mail address)
- hours of operation
- map and directions (Directions should include all the commonly traveled routes to the library.)
- staff (director and department heads, with direct contact information)
- list and brief description of services, organized by age group or format or both
- program and events schedule or calendar
- Internet and computer access guidelines
- meeting room policy and sign-up procedures
- frequently asked questions: library card registration, renewing materials, and so on

The home page of the Thomas Memorial Library, located in Cape Elizabeth, Maine, provides an excellent example of a well-organized, uncluttered web design (see figure 4.1). The library received the EBSCO Excellence in Small and/or Rural Public Library Service Award in 2008.

THE PHYSICAL LIBRARY

As for the library's physical presence, the best approach for evaluating how it is positioned is to conduct an observational activity called "Walk Into the Library for the First Time." Staff can become so accustomed to their surroundings that they forget how the average or occasional visitor views the various components of the library's layout. What may appear logical and obvious from a staff service-desk perspective may strike library users as haphazard and ambiguous.

But before we walk into the library, let's take an external inventory. How does your facility stack up against these guidelines?

Directional signs are posted in prominent locations, such as major intersections, in the vicinity of the library (see figure 4.2).

The *exterior architectural features* clearly identify the building as a library. A "landmark" sign, placed at the access point to the main entrance, is clearly visible as people approach the library. If space and design allow, the sign includes the library's hours of operation.

The library provides convenient and sufficient *off-street parking,* with the minimum number of handicapped stalls as required by law. Generally speaking, a library should provide one parking space for every 400 square feet of building space. In

FIGURE 4.1 : Homepage of the Thomas Memorial Library

Homepage of the Thomas Memorial Library, Cape Elizabeth, Maine, recipient of the 2008 EBSCO Excellence in Small and/or Rural Public Library Service Award.

other words, the parking lot for a 16,000-square-foot facility offers no less than forty parking spaces.

The library's *name* and its *hours of operation* are prominently displayed at the main entrance to the facility.

Let's continue our observations as we enter the library proper. Often, the first space that people encounter is a vestibule or lobby.

The library's immediate entryway provides a bulletin board and shelving for the display of library activities and community events. The area remains free of clutter.

FIGURE 4.2 : City of Monona, Wisconsin, signage

If space permits, a prominently placed monitor offers a series of slides highlighting library programs and services, the day's meeting room schedule, and other pertinent information.

Now we're in the library proper.

The library's public service space has a decidedly welcoming feel to it. When possible, and at a minimum, staff members acknowledge patrons entering the library with eye contact and a smile. The placement of the library's primary service desk determines how effectively this practice may be used.

The library provides clearly visible "identification" signage—for example, "Adult Fiction," "Teen Area," "Storytime Room." A large floor plan designates the location of the various collections, service desks, seating areas, public access computers, and special use spaces. Strategically placed "theme," or "wayfinding," signage leads patrons to specific locations within the library.

Staff members at service desks appear approachable and ready to provide assistance. They will occasionally move away from the desk to help patrons find what they need.

Areas designated for adults, teens, and children are furnished appropriately, with various styles of seating and accessible shelving.

Establishing a Signage Hierarchy in the Library

Level One: Section Identification
- Text-based signs should be visible from the main path through the library.

Level Two: Theme
- Images provide immediately accessible information for the viewer; use them to convey the topics and content of the section.
- Theme signage should be visible from outside the section in order to attract patrons.

Level Three: Dewey Identification
- Keep the Dewey signage on the ends of the stacks, as patrons know where to look for this information.

Level Four: Shelf Talk
- Face out titles on the shelves; use framed easel signs to direct readers to similar titles.

Source: Adapted from *Envirosell Final Report for the Metropolitan Library System* (New York: Envirosell, 2008), www.mls.lib.il.us/consulting/pdf/EnvirosellFinalReport.pdf.

SAFETY ISSUES

According to Murphy's Law, a building emergency is certain to occur when the library director is elsewhere, most likely at a meeting twenty miles away or on vacation in another state. In addition, something will always go wrong when the least senior supervisor has been left in charge.

So what is a staff member to do when a patron approaches the desk and announces, "The toilet in the women's restroom has overflowed"?

Or a member of the local chapter of the AAUW, a group that always donates so generously to the library each year, complains that the meeting room is much too cold. "We haven't been able to take off our coats," she adds.

Or the tornado siren sounds, and it's not at the time of its weekly test.

An emergency procedures manual should be accessible from all staff computers. As backup, manuals should also be available in ring-bound notebooks kept within easy reach at service

Emergency Services Checklist

Emergency contacts	Organization/contact person(s)	Phone (day/night)
Ambulance		
Fire department		
Police/sheriff's department		
Telephone company		
Utility company		
Locksmith		
Plumber		
Electrician		
Computer network support		
Exterminator/animal control		
Janitorial service		
Attorney		

To this list you should attach a floor plan of your library, with the following locations listed and marked:

- main water shutoff valve
- sprinkler shutoff valve
- electrical box
- main gas shutoff valve
- HVAC controls
- fire extinguishers
- first aid kits

desks and in supervisors' offices (for when the power goes out). At a minimum, the manual should contain the following information.

BAD WEATHER CLOSING PROCEDURE

Generally speaking, the library director determines whether to open or close the library in the event of inclement weather. In certain situations, officials may strongly encourage all municipal departments to close. If the decision is made before the library is scheduled to open, employees scheduled to work that day must be notified. In addition, the following actions are recommended:

- Contact local media.
- Contact neighboring libraries and library system headquarters (where appropriate).

- Change message on library's voice mail to indicate reason for closing.
- Post announcement on library's home page.
- Post announcement at entrance to library (when possible).

In each case, try to indicate when the library will reopen.

This section of your emergency procedures manual should also provide a detailed description of staff responsibilities during *tornado watches and warnings,* particularly in regard to clearing the public services areas of the library and assisting unaccompanied children. Many states have a Tornado and/or Severe Weather Awareness Week that includes a drill with mock watches and warnings. Library staff members are well-advised to participate in these events.

Especially in areas where severe storms are common, libraries should have a NOAA (National Oceanic and Atmospheric Administration) weather radio on hand in order to receive weather warnings and forecasts from the National Weather Service. The radio should have a battery backup and a tone alert feature that sounds when a watch or warning is issued.

FIRE ALARMS

Whenever a fire alarm sounds, false or otherwise, staff must ensure that there is a calm and orderly clearing of the building. In multistoried facilities, do not allow the use of elevators. An announcement should be made over the library's public-address system, if one is available. Once outside, people should be directed away from the building in order to provide unhindered access for emergency personnel. Nobody should be within one hundred feet of the building.

In the case of a containable fire, such as trash burning in a wastebasket, ignited food in the microwave, and the like, the staff member who discovers it should attempt to put it out. All staff members should know the location of the fire extinguishers in the library.

This section of the emergency procedures manual should include a floor plan that clearly indicates the locations of fire alarms and fire extinguishers throughout the library.

EMERGENCY CLOSING PROCEDURE

Some incidents may be classified as emergency situations requiring the library to be closed or not to open until the necessary corrective action is taken.

WHAT TO LISTEN FOR: Severe Weather Watches vs. Warnings

Tornado watch. Tornadoes are possible in your area. Remain alert for approaching storms.

Tornado warning. A tornado has been sighted or indicated by weather radar. If a tornado warning is issued for your area and the sky becomes threatening, move to your predesignated place of safety.

Severe thunderstorm watch. Severe thunderstorms are possible in your area.

Severe thunderstorm warning. Severe thunderstorms are occurring.

Source: NOAA National Severe Storms Laboratory.

- Interior temperature of the building is outside the comfort zone.
- The building is without electrical power.
- Severe damage has occurred to the building as the result of a natural or other disaster.
- There is an insufficient number of staff to operate the library.

BUILDING SYSTEMS AND EQUIPMENT MALFUNCTIONS

These types of emergencies include any situation that requires prompt attention but does not interfere with the operation of the library—that is, does not require the library to close. Examples of such malfunctions include but are certainly not limited to the following:

- inoperative phone system
- faulty plumbing
- partial power outage/flickering lights
- noticeable but still tolerable change in the temperature of the building's interior
- elevator malfunction
- security system malfunction
- inoperable locks
- entry/exit doors that don't close securely
- broken windows

This section of the emergency procedures manual should provide an approved list of business names and contact information for situations that cannot be resolved by library staff. In addition, this section should contain a floor plan with clearly marked, color-coded locations of the library's mechanical equipment—specifically, water main shutoff valves, electrical cutoff switch, gas main shutoff, and heating and cooling controls, including all thermostats.

To ensure prompt attention by staff, step-by-step directions for both shutoff and start-up procedures should be posted near the valves and/or switches.

INAPPROPRIATE BEHAVIOR AND PROBLEM PATRONS

On occasion, the issue of safety involves efforts to preserve a welcoming, comforting atmosphere in the library and ensure that equitable access to services and materials is maintained for all.

Inappropriate behavior includes any activity that disturbs others, interferes with library operations, or damages the building or its furnishings. More generally, it also encompasses rudeness, profanity, or any other behavior generally considered unacceptable in a public place.

Dealing with problem patrons is probably the most stressful aspect of working in a library. For that reason, staff members must be given the necessary training and guidelines to deal effectively with these situations.

Dealing with Problem Patrons

1. Restate the policy or procedure that needs to be observed. (Example: "It is the library's policy to renew materials twice. I'm sorry, but I won't be able to renew this item for you again." "It's the library policy to charge $1 to replace a lost library card.")

2. Speak in a clear, firm, but friendly voice. If the patron is persistent, do not argue or show anger. Keep a pleasant disposition and maintain eye contact.

3. At a service desk when others are waiting to check out, refer the person to a supervisor. ("There are other people waiting to check out. Let me have _____ follow up on your concern.")

4. If the encounter begins to escalate, refer the patron to the library director or the staff member in charge. ("I'm sure the library director would be interested in hearing your concerns.") A change of venue is often helpful.

5. If the patron exhibits violent behavior or the potential for violent behavior, a staff member should call 911 immediately.

6. If the patron becomes abusive or continues to be uncooperative, attempt to excuse yourself and notify the library director or staff member in charge of the need for assistance.

7. The library director or staff member in charge should discuss the situation with the problem patron out of the public eye.

Staff members who are working in the vicinity of a problem patron encounter should be prepared to act when the situation requires it. This may include offering assistance or making the 911 call. In each case, an incident report should be written up and shared with all appropriate staff.

RENOVATION, EXPANSION, NEW CONSTRUCTION

Whether it's a 30,000-square-foot new facility or a 3,000-square-foot remodeling of a portion of your present building, the key to success in any library construction project, big or small, is careful planning that involves the library board, staff, and local officials.

Anders C. Dahlgren, president of Library Planning Associates, Inc., provides an informative, well-organized starting point. His planning guide, *Public Library Space Needs: A Planning Outline/2009* (Wisconsin Department of Public Instruction), defines six broad areas of library space that must be considered during any library construction project. Each element addresses a specific area of the library's service program that, taken as a whole, helps to ensure that the community's needs are well met.

1. *Collection space*—books, periodicals, audiovisual materials, digital resources

2. *Reader seating space*—from the traditional array of tables, carrels, and lounge chairs to more contemporary touches such as diner booths, rocking chairs, cushions, and pouffes

3. *Staff work space*—service desks, public workstations, nonpublic workstations and offices

Template for Incident Report

Date and time of incident:	
Subject (such as a problem patron's name):	
Person making report:	
Staff present:	
Location of incident:	
Description of incident:	
Comments received from witnesses:	
Action taken by staff:	
Follow-up requested/taken:	

4. *Meeting room space*—general program space, conference room, storytime room, computer lab

5. *Special use space*—small-group study rooms, staff lounge/break room, photocopier, microform reader/printer, café, self-checkout operations and self-service holds

6. *Nonassignable space*—furnace room, janitor's closet, telecommunications room, storage rooms, vestibule, corridors, stairwells, elevator shafts, restrooms

For each section, Dahlgren provides guidelines and formulas for determining the amount of space that is recommended based on the library's service design population—that is, the population the library is expected to serve over a twenty-year planning time frame.

Questions to Answer Before Selecting an Architect
(no matter the size of the project)

Experience/Previous Work
- What other libraries has the architect worked on?
- What did you learn about the design and construction of these libraries during site visits and/or discussions with key staff?

Ability to Work with Client
- Is the architect registered to practice in your state?
- Does the architectural firm have the resources and time to complete your project?

Planning and Design
- Will the architect use charrettes [collaborative planning sessions conducted with all stakeholders present] to gather input?
- Will the architect work alone or with a design team?
- Who are the members of the design team? (examples: landscape architect; civil, structural, mechanical, electrical engineers; interior designer)

Communication
- Does the architect have good listening, written, and oral presentation skills?
- Will the architect work with all stakeholders in the project? (board, staff, public, local officials)
- Does the architect have the political skills necessary to listen and respond to the concerns of various stakeholders?

Source: Adapted from a document provided by the New Jersey State Library.

BUILDING PROGRAM STATEMENT

A library's building program statement serves dual, equally important purposes. First, it describes in considerable detail the functional needs of the project, such as service points, collections, public seating, and staff workspace. More critically, the document reflects the fact that the library board and staff have articulated a clear vision of what they want to accomplish.

Second, a building program statement conveys a set of well-organized, comprehensive, and unambiguous instructions to the architect. In other words, it contains all the information that is required for the design development portion of the project.

A typical building program statement should contain all the following elements:

An introductory statement provides a description of the library's service area, including its present and future demographic characteristics. If appropriate, a brief history may be included, especially if it has some bearing on the architectural design. Specific planning concepts that have guided the board and staff throughout the development of the building program statement—those related to special collections, technology, and resource sharing, for example—should be described concisely in this section.

A summary statement of the library's resources—that is, materials and services to be provided for all ages and circumstances within the facility—needs to include collections (print, audiovisual, and digital—all formats and subdivisions), seating (numbers, type, purpose, age-appropriateness), special features for groups (meeting, study, storytime rooms), and staff work areas (public, nonpublic, purpose).

General design considerations include such topics as code requirements, site considerations (when appropriate), access requirements (Americans with Disabilities Act, for example), parking needs, interior design and furniture selection, technology requirements, lighting, maintenance, and security.

A detailed description of each department, or functional area, of the library—adult fiction, children's area, circulation desk—comprises the bulk of the building program statement. For each area, the following questions are answered.

- How much square footage is required?
- How many library staff members and users need to be accommodated in this area?
- What equipment is located here?
- What activities take place here?
- What specific architectural features are required: ambiance, lighting, flooring, access?
- What types of furnishings are located here?
- How should this space be designed in relation to other areas of the library?
- What materials are shelved/displayed here?

ACCESS TO TECHNOLOGY

By the year 2000, public access to the Internet was already well established in libraries in the United States. At that time, 94.5 percent of all public libraries—urban, suburban, and rural—offered this service.[1] Fewer rural libraries (91.9 percent) were connected, however. The average number of public access computers provided varied by the metropolitan status of the library's service area: urban (17), suburban (9), and rural (5). Nearly a decade later, 98.7 percent of U.S. public libraries offered public access to the Internet. At the same time, the average number of computers provided by libraries increased by one-third.[2]

Several challenges and concerns emerged from the 2009 ALA/Gates Foundation study, *Public Libraries and the Internet,* as reflected in the following statistics:

Of all public libraries, 71.4 percent reported that they were the only area provider of free public Internet and computer access. This figure increased to 78.6 percent in rural libraries.

Less than 20 percent of libraries reported that a sufficient number of computer workstations were always available.

LIBRARY AREA: Children's/Family Area

Size
1,298 sq. ft.

Occupancy
Staff: 2
Public: 16
Daily Uses: Intermittent whenever the library is open

Equipment
Wall clock, floor thermostat, room thermostat, fire extinguisher, smoke detector, emergency lights, emergency alarm. One workstation for Children's Librarian with computer, flat screen monitor, mouse and keyboard, and telephone.

Activities
Parents reading to small children, children playing and browsing library materials. Open area of 200 square feet could accommodate both storytelling and children's play area.

Architectural Features (ambiance, lighting requirements, flooring, access to area)
Preschool area should be bright with indirect but high lighting. Heated flooring was installed in this room in 2008. Bookshelves should be no higher than four shelves with wall space retained for exhibits and displays. Sound absorbing materials should be built into the design of the room to lower the decibel level. The area should be designed to contain the children with easy supervision of the entranceway. The storytelling area should have adjustable lighting. A craft area could be incorporated with very easily cleanable flooring and walls, and a sink for clean-up. Stacks should be no more than four shelves high, three preferred.

Furnishings
Total seats:
    Table: 2 small child-sized with 8 chairs
    Lounge: 1 loveseat for adult to read with child, 1 large chair, 4 alternate chairs for children, 5 informal beanbag chairs
    Staff: 1 staff desk and chair
    1 computer station

Proximities
Near: Youth room, family restroom, large storage closet for children's crafts
Away from: adult traffic lanes through library
In sight of: Youth room service desk

Books
Picture; Beginning Readers; Easy Readers, Easy NF

Nonbook Materials
Kit/Audio Books; Puzzles/Toys; Magazines

Source: Goffstown (New Hampshire) Public Library Building Program, Cheryl Bryan Consulting.

Nearly 40 percent of all libraries (49.2 percent of rural libraries) reported that they did not have a workstation replacement or addition schedule.

The two primary factors determining workstation addition decisions were cost and space limitations. Not surprisingly, cost factors were also the biggest influence in hardware replacement decisions. When repairs were required, nearly 50 percent of the computers were out of service for two or more days.

In 47.2 percent of rural libraries, the director was the main source of IT and computer support. And if the director couldn't fix it, an outside vendor or contractor was most likely to be used (33.8 percent). System-level IT staff support was most likely to occur in urban libraries (72.2 percent).

Laptops are a very effective solution for the issues of cost and space, while also expanding the reach of a library's existing network. Laptop computers provide a flexible solution in smaller buildings where adding another designated workstation is not an option and in older buildings that present challenges to the installation of traditional network wiring. Unlike desktop computers, laptops may be checked out and taken to carrels, study rooms, or other "off-the-beaten-path" locations within the library. According to a 2007 Web4lib survey, librarians affirmed the overwhelming popularity of laptops for patron use but did note the added responsibility of maintaining more equipment.

If operating funds are not available to purchase computers, library staff should investigate other avenues of support, such as Friends of the Library groups, fund-raising, unrestricted gifts, local businesses, foundations, and grants. The Bill and Melinda Gates Foundation, for example, has provided millions of dollars to "support efforts to supply and sustain free public access to computers and the Internet through local public libraries."[3]

Dos and Don'ts for Lending Laptops for In-Library Use

The Middleton (Wisconsin) Public Library has provided laptops to check out for in-library use since 2007. Sarah Hartman, Middleton's technical services librarian, offers suggestions for those libraries planning to offer this service.

Dos

- Do have a formal, written policy and procedures in place. Educate staff.
- Do make your policies clear to patrons. Consider a laptop borrower agreement.
- Do protect laptops with ownership stickers, engraving, RFID (radio-frequency identification), or tattle tape.
- Do publicize the service and ask for staff and patron feedback.

Don'ts

- Don't overspend. Cheaper laptops are more than adequate for most users' needs.
- Don't rely solely on battery power. Provide power cables and outlets.
- Don't forget the mice for patrons uncomfortable with or unable to use touch pads.
- Don't leave circulating laptops unfiltered if you must comply with CIPA (Children's Internet Protection Act).

TECHNOLOGY COMPETENCIES

Many libraries and library agencies have developed technology competencies as part of their staff development activities. These guidelines may be categorized in a variety of ways, including level of staffing (page, clerk, library assistant, professional librarian) and degree of responsibility (general to specialized). Supervisors find them especially useful when creating or revising position descriptions, conducting performance evaluations, and helping staff adapt to new technologies.

The State Library of North Carolina, for example, has developed a tiered approach to technology competencies.[4]

Level I: For all staff members.

Level II: For staff who work with the public, such as service desk and formal computer instruction responsibilities.

Level III: For staff who are assigned specialized responsibilities, such as hardware troubleshooting and repair, network management, and virtual reference.

Within each level, staff members are encouraged to develop competencies in specific areas of library-related technology.

Level I examples:

- Terminology: understanding basic vocabulary and recognizing standard acronyms
- Hardware skills: having a basic knowledge of computer use (powering on and off; using a mouse, keyboard, and function keys) and learning basic printer skills (loading paper, changing a cartridge, clearing jams)
- Operating system skills: launching applications from desktop or menu, managing folders and files
- Basic Internet skills: using navigational buttons, performing basic searches, entering URLs, scrolling, searching for text
- E-mail skills: composing, storing, retrieving, and sorting messages; attaching a file and opening an attachment

In addition to the core list of technology competencies, Level II library employees are expected to gain knowledge and develop skills in areas related to their public-service responsibilities. These enhanced abilities include having a thorough knowledge of workstation management and circulation software, developing advanced search strategies for public access catalogs (including a familiarity with all online resources available through regional and statewide consortia), using social networks and other so-called Web 2.0 applications, and participating in online discussion groups.

In small public libraries, a Level III employee is likely to be a staff member of a library system or resource library—someone who is not necessarily available at a moment's notice, in other words. Competencies at this level are generally associated with a library's information technology operations: web page creation and maintenance, audiovisual equipment use, virtual/chat reference, all levels of computer security, and technical support.

NOTES

1. John Carlo Bertot and Charles R. McClure, *Public Libraries and the Internet 2000: Summary Findings and Data Tables* (Washington, DC: National Commission on Libraries and Information Science, 2000).
2. John Carlo Bertot, Charles R. McClure, Carla B. Wright, Elise Jensen, and Susan Thomas, *Public Libraries and the Internet 2009: Study Results and Findings.* For: The American Library Association and the Bill and Melinda Gates Foundation, http://www.ii.fsu.edu/content/view/full/17025.
3. Bill and Melinda Gates Foundation, www.gatesfoundation.org/Pages/home.aspx.
4. State Library of North Carolina, "Technology Competencies for Libraries in North Carolina," 2007, http://statelibrary.ncdcr.gov/ce/images/Competencies.pdf.

CHAPTER FIVE

COLLECTION MANAGEMENT

THE WORD *library* dates from the fourteenth century and referred to a collection of writings—first manuscripts and documents, and later books. Check the word in a dictionary and you'll find something like this definition from *Merriam-Webster: a place in which literary, musical, artistic, or reference materials (as books, manuscripts, recordings, or films) are kept for use but not for sale; a collection of such materials.* It is safe to say that for many centuries the word referred to the collection and the room or building that housed it, rather than the services and programs that complement the collection and are integral parts of public library service. Nevertheless, management of the collection remains a major part of managing the library as a whole.

The term *collection management* has come to replace what was commonly known as collection development because so much more than development or selection is involved. Collection management involves the identification, selection, acquisition, and evaluation of a collection of library resources (e.g., print materials, audiovisual materials, electronic resources) for a community of users, but also includes writing collection policies, weeding the collection, dealing with challenges to materials, monitoring the condition of materials, and making decisions about preservation and conservation.

There are many classic works on collection development that focus on the book selection aspect. Indeed, Lionel McColvin's classic work, *The Theory of Book Selection for Public Libraries*, begins, "Book selection is the first task of librarianship. It precedes all other processes—cataloguing, classification, or administration—and it is the most important."[1] However, book selection, although one of the most important aspects of library work, does not really precede all other processes, but, rather, must follow the understanding of the library's mission and community needs. The collection manager has to know something not only about the library's users and potential users but also about trends in publishing and formats (think about how quickly DVDs have become popular), about other sources of information, and about changes in user behavior.

Many of the classic twentieth-century works on collection development were concerned with the question of whether to emphasize the quality of the materials to raise literary awareness and educate and enlighten a community, or to focus on demand and potential use to satisfy the needs and wants of the public that is funding the purchases. They cautioned librarians to "strive to get the best title on any subject, but do not hesitate to add a mediocre title that will be read rather than a superior title that will be unread" and "use restraint in responding to demands of aggressive patrons, and recognize the inarticulate patron's demands."[2] Although the context for selection decisions may have changed greatly since these classic works first appeared (audiovisual and electronic formats and participation in shared resource systems, for example), many of their basic criteria for selection are still applicable and are worth examining. Helen Haines, in her 1935 classic work, *Living with Books*, summarized "certain principles that are commonly accepted as fundamental in book selection."[3]

Jumping ahead a few decades, Robert Broadus, in *Selecting Materials for Libraries*, identified new factors to consider in anticipating demand, including the impact of publicity (for example, an author interviewed on radio or television, or a movie version of a book) and possible opposition to a title (as controversy will stimulate demand).[4] But he, too, urged keeping a reasonably high percentage of standards and classics in the collection, saying that even if they are not

---

Helen Haines—*Living with Books* (1935)

1. Study your community and know its general and special characteristics, racial elements, chief activities, and reading interests.

2. Be familiar with subjects of present interest, general, national, and local.

3. Represent in book selection all subjects that apply to community conditions and that reflect community interests.

4. Make your collection of local history as extensive and useful as possible.

5. Provide for all organized groups whose activities or interests can be related to books.

6. Provide materials for both actual and potential readers by satisfying so far as possible existent demands and anticipating demands foreshadowed by events, conditions, or increasing use of the library.

7. Avoid selection of books for which no demand is evident, and supersede books that have definitely outlived their usefulness.

8. Remember that the great works of literature are foundation stones in the library's own structure and therefore select some books of permanent value regardless of whether or not they will be widely used.

9. Maintain impartiality in selection; favor no special hobbies or opinions; in controversial or sectarian subjects, gifts may be accepted when purchase may be undesirable.

Source: Helen Haines, *Living with Books* (New York: Columbia University Press, 1935).

extensively used, they have public relations value in dealing with groups that have concerns about the quality of the collection.

When Broadus was writing, it was still something of a novelty to say that "libraries are more than books." Now the selector must not only grapple with the question of demand versus quality but also decide how to allocate among various formats. In the small library, a single person may be responsible for selection of adult, teen, and children's fiction and nonfiction (in print and in audio format), periodicals, DVDs, electronic reference works, and perhaps downloadable digital material. A collection development and materials selection policy helps selectors to work consistently toward building a collection that is related to the long- and short-range needs of all parts of the community rather than accumulating materials randomly. A policy helps set standards for the selection and weeding of materials, helps minimize personal bias by selectors, serves as a training tool to ease transition from one librarian to the next, informs the public of the scope of the collection and the basis for selection and withdrawal decisions, and serves as a tool to handle complaints or requests for reconsideration of material. As with any other library policy, it should be approved by the board and be reviewed regularly and updated in response to changing needs.

A collection development policy includes a description of the institution and its clientele and an overview of the collection, which may include some history and describe its broad areas of emphasis. If part of the library collection is housed at another location, such as a local school or nursing home, this also should be noted. The policy should include information on the formats and types of materials collected by the library (or specifically excluded from the library's scope) and selection criteria for these, and may also have explicit guidelines for deselection, commonly known as weeding. The policy may also offer guidelines for preservation, replacement, and storage decisions; acquisitions matters such as standing or blanket orders; multiple copies; and dealing with gifts. It should also provide a policy and procedure for requests for reconsideration of library materials.

Why does the policy need to spell out the formats and types of materials collected (or excluded)? This specificity not only guides the selectors but also helps to answer patron questions. *Why do/don't you have the latest movies on DVD? Could the library subscribe to online genealogical resources? Would the library buy games and graphic novels suggested by teen patrons? Can you get these out-of-print titles listed in our homeschooling curriculum? My grandparents only read Spanish, and I'd like to bring them large-print materials—are there any?*

SELECTION CRITERIA

So is selection an art or a science? A combination of skill, knowledge of both the library's holdings and the library's users, and the right selection tools is required to select appropriate library materials that meet the community's needs. A skilled selector keeps up with what is happening in the community, in the publishing industry, and in the world at large. Actively evaluating the collection and its use statistics, reading a variety of reviews, and looking at the catalogs of other libraries help to increase the selector's knowledge base. There are some general criteria for selection, which include subject matter, potential use, relation to the collection, and cost.

Collections

No small library collects all of these, but here are some examples.

Books
- Adults, children, teens
- Circulating, reference
- Print: hardcover, paperback, large print
- Digital: MP3, downloadable

Periodicals
- Adults, children, teens
- Magazines, newspapers
- Current and back issues (print and microforms)

Audiovisual materials
- Adults, children, teens
- Formats: tape, disc, preloaded, downloadable
- Type: movies, music, audiobooks, foreign language, games, etc.

Realia (miscellaneous items)
- Equipment (audiovisual, energy meters, tools, etc.)
- Art prints/reproductions
- Maps
- Toys, board games

Sample Selection Criteria

Materials are selected for the library's collection to meet the cultural, informational, educational, and recreational needs of the residents of the community. Selectors attempt to choose materials that will build a balanced collection which includes a range of viewpoints and opinions. The main elements considered in the selection of materials are:

- The individual merit of each item (which may include literary merit, lasting value, accuracy, authoritativeness, timeliness), as determined by reviews, reputation of author (or publisher, in certain areas), and/or hands-on examination. Nonbook formats may also be evaluated for technical or production quality and ease of use, where appropriate.
- Popular appeal, as determined by patron demand, reputation of author, circulation history of similar materials, or promotion/discussion of the title in public media
- Appropriateness of material for the library's clientele. This refers not to the subject matter but to the scope or depth of the treatment of a topic. For example, there is a tremendous amount of health information available, but a public library selector is likely to seek out materials meant for patients and consumers, rather than for medical researchers or health practitioners.
- Existing library holdings, both in this library and in other area libraries
- Price

Reviews are a major source of information about new materials. The primary sources of reviews used by this library are

- *Library Journal*
- *New York Times Book Review*
- *Publishers Weekly*
- *Booklist*
- *Book Links*
- *AudioFile*
- *CCBC Choices*

Publishers' catalogs and promotional materials, patron suggestions, professional publications of recommended titles, and specialized book blogs are also used as selection tools.

Selection Criteria for Nonbook Material

Here are some questions to consider in developing selection policies for various formats.

Video/DVD

- How will this format support library goals?
- Should we purchase a wide variety or only certain genres? Educational films? Popular? Will MPAA (Motion Picture Association of America) ratings be a consideration? What languages will we collect in?
- Should we consider leasing new feature films and offering a rental collection?
- How will films be used? Do we need to get a public performance license?
- How durable is the product?

Audiobooks

- How will this format support library goals?
- Should we purchase a wide variety or only certain genres? Popular books? Works for learning languages?
- What format will we purchase (CD, downloadable)? Will we replace works on cassette tapes?
- Will we purchase abridged versions that are often available or complete works only?
- What is the overall quality of the performance?
- How durable is the product?

Newspapers

- Do we need multiple subscriptions for browsing of current issues?
- Can the local newspaper be obtained/preserved on microfilm?
- Is there an index to the local newspaper?
- How long will back issues be kept?

BASIC SELECTION QUESTIONS

- How does this title fit into the collection development policy for this subject?
- How important is the title in relationship to other works already owned by the library on this subject?
- Is there a level of use that would justify the acquisition?
- Do we need more than one copy? How many?
- Is it part of a series? Do we have the rest of the series?
- Are there collaborative reasons for acquiring this title?
- How responsive will we be with regard to popular materials?
- Is there a local connection (author, small press, subject matter)?

Selection criteria may vary according to collection area, genre, and format, but generally reflect both the intrinsic merits of the works and the need for those works to improve the collection.

How important are the following considerations in determining what you buy? Patron recommendations? Staff recommendations? Lack of anything else in the collection on a particular

Is There a Magic Formula?

In her first few years as library director, Rose Martin allocated the collection budget the same way her predecessor had done it: periodicals, reference, and audiovisual materials each received a fixed percentage of the materials budget, and the remainder became the book budget. This was then divided among different types of materials based on the previous year's circulation figures. After a few years, Rose wondered if this made sense. After all, some categories of books cost more than others, so fewer books were purchased in those categories even if the circulation figures implied good demand for the category. Conversely, paperback genre fiction, which was relatively inexpensive, was being acquired in disproportionately large numbers, although these items weren't very durable and didn't particularly add enduring value to the library's collection.

Rose was also ready to hand off selection duties for children's materials to her assistant, who had been increasingly involved in the library's programming for children. Her assistant wondered if in addition to the budget amount she would have to spend in each juvenile category, she could get an idea of approximately how many books she could buy in a year. Was there perhaps another kind of formula they could use to allocate the book budget?

The library materials budget was just under $50,000, of which $32,000 was earmarked for the circulating book collection. Rose ran a report to get the circulation percentages for the various categories, and estimated the average price of materials in each category:

Code	Category	Percentage of circulation	Average price
P	Picture books	12	$12
J	Juvenile fiction	9	$10
JN	Juvenile nonfiction	10	$12
F	Adult general fiction	23	$13
G	Genre fiction (mysteries, sci-fi, romance)	17	$ 8
NF	General nonfiction	29	$15

Based simply on circulation percentages, the allocations would look like this:

P = $3,840   J = $2,880   JN = $3,200   F = $7,360   G = $5,440   NF = $9,280

However, it is possible to create an indexed formula that takes into account both the circulation percentage and the average price, yielding an approximate number of books per category. Are you ready for some algebra?

$$[P\%(P\$)x] + [J\%(J\$)x] + [JN\%(JN\$)x] + [F\%(F\$)x] + [G\%(G\$)x] + [NF\%(NF\$)x] = \text{Total budget for these categories}$$

In other words, for each category, take the circulation percentage per code, multiplied by the average price, multiplied by x. Add those amounts for all categories and solve for x:

Step One: $[12(12)x] + [9(10)x] + [10(12)x] + [23(13)x] + [17(8)x] + [29(15)x] = 32,000$

Step Two: $144x + 90x + 120x + 299x + 136x + 435x = 32,000$

Step Three: $1,224x = 32,000$

Step Four: $x = 32,000/1,224$, therefore $x = 26.14$

In the following table, the formula represents the circulation percentage multiplied by x, which yields the approximate number of items that can be purchased in each category. The budget amounts now reflect the average price of books in the category.

Code	Category	Formula	Number of items	New budget amount
P	Picture books	12 × 26.14	314	$ 3,764
J	Juvenile fiction	9 × 26.14	235	$ 2,353
JN	Juvenile nonfiction	10 × 26.14	261	$ 3,137
F	Adult general fiction	23 × 26.14	601	$ 7,816
G	Genre fiction (mysteries, sci-fi, etc.)	17 × 26.14	444	$ 3,555
NF	General nonfiction	29 × 26.14	758	$11,371

subject? To what extent do you use reviews in professional library journals? Reviews in general interest publications? Publishers' catalogs?

The collection budget may appear as a single item in the line-item budget, but the library manager must decide how to allocate that budget into various categories such as adult fiction, adult nonfiction, juvenile fiction, juvenile nonfiction, periodicals, reference works, audiobooks, and DVDs. Although it may be tempting to base the allocations on either the previous budget or the circulation percentages for each category, there are actually many factors to consider, and it's important to balance circulation and patron requests with other concerns when making these allocations. Regular evaluation of the use of the collection can provide data to help make these allocations.

GIFTS

Many people like to get rid of their old books by donating them to the library. Policies on gift acceptance range from "we don't accept any gift" to "we will take anything." It all depends on how the librarians view the best interests of the library. A comprehensive gift policy should cover the conditions under which the library will accept or reject gifts. The procedures for handling gifts may include how donations are acknowledged, whether there will be donor recognition (such as book plates for books donated in someone's honor), and methods of disposal of unwanted items.

If an individual or group decides to donate materials with the expectation that these materials will become part of the library's collection, the librarian should first consider if the items meet selection criteria and if they will actually be used by the community. (There may be some situations where a donation of materials from a local author or potential major donor is accepted for the collection even though the use is not likely to be significant, because the library wants to maintain good relations with that donor.) Donors sometimes offer gifts with strings attached, such as requesting that the donated materials be kept together or kept indefinitely

---

Sample Patron Handout on Book Donations

Thinking about donating your used books?

Things we need:

- Local history materials from this county—high school yearbooks, maps, business and family histories, photos of buildings
- Recent best sellers
- "Classics" in good condition

Help us out:

- Call first if you have more than one or two cartons.
- Bring books in boxes or shopping bags to the side of the checkout desk.

Things we can't even give away at our book sale:

- Books in poor condition (brittle pages, musty smell, torn covers)
- Textbooks older than two years
- Dated information (old computer manuals, almanacs, etc.)
- Magazines (except for cooking and crafts)

If you would like a receipt for tax purposes, please count the books you are donating and include that with your name and address. We will send you a dated receipt for the number of items donated. The library does not assess the value.

---

or both. Conditions such as these may be reason to reject a gift, since they could lead to space or preservation issues in the future. Most policies will specify that books not needed by the library may be sold or otherwise disposed of, and many donors are happy to have items go into the library book sale.

Donors frequently do not have a realistic idea of the usefulness or value of books they intend to donate. (A used book that is not distinguished by its edition, provenance, binding, or overall condition generally has a fairly modest value. Even if it is pretty old it is not necessarily valuable.) Many donors will also be interested in potentially taking a deduction from their annual income tax. A 1993 law requires people donating money or property to a charity to get a written receipt for each donation of $250 or more. Donors must get the receipt before taking a deduction for the donation. In most cases the librarian will not do the valuation of the books but may supply a receipt indicating the number of books or, in the case of a large donation, the number of cartons.

CIRCULATION POLICY

Because the collection of a public library is meant primarily for lending, written circulation policies and procedures are part of managing the collection. These should establish the loan period for different types of materials and set procedures for the issuing of library cards, dealing with lost or forgotten cards, and handling fines or replacement charges. The policy regarding confidentiality of library records should also be stated. This policy should be written in accordance with any applicable state statute and should be available on request to anyone who wonders about the privacy of library records. Once a borrowed item has been checked back in, most public libraries do not keep records of what individuals have borrowed and therefore cannot compromise users' privacy.

COLLECTION EVALUATION, WEEDING, AND PRESERVATION

Collection development doesn't stop with the selection process. Although the acquisition of new materials keeps a collection up-to-date, it is important to evaluate the collection on a regular basis to determine whether the library's holdings are satisfying the various needs of the user community. What are some of the benefits of an evaluation or assessment process? The information gathered provides a tool for analyzing selection decisions and can provide the rationale for weeding a collection (or replacing or repairing worn materials). The assessment data should feed into the budget process, if there are areas that seem weak or are so heavily used that the library is not meeting demand.

There are two approaches to evaluating a collection: collection-centered and user-centered. Collection-centered techniques look at the collection by itself—the size, scope, depth, condition. This evaluation might be done in comparison to the holdings of other libraries of similar size. How does your collection hold up in terms of number of volumes, median copyright date, or holdings from recommended lists? Information can also be shared if you are cooperating with other libraries in purchasing materials. Of course, numbers alone won't tell you if this is the *right* collection for your users.

User-centered techniques focus on whether and how often materials are being used. It is also useful to look at *who* is using your collection—not by patron name, but by category. For example, are teens using the young adult collection? Are many of the items that circulate coming from other libraries in a shared resource system? Table 5.1 compares various methods for evaluating the collection. They all have advantages and disadvantages, so a combination of techniques must be employed to get a good picture of the quality and vitality of a collection. A collection review can help bring the library's holdings into better alignment with the library's mission and collection policy by highlighting the areas that really do support the mission and those that are less relevant to it and are merely taking up shelf space.

A collection that is up-to-date, easy to browse, and appealing to users can only be maintained through a continual evaluation process that includes withdrawal of some materials, either for lack of use or poor condition. Although a continuous review may sound time-consuming, in a small library it really is possible to review for weeding, preservation, and replacement at the same time by looking over one area of the shelves each week and by noting the condition of borrowed material as it is returned. Items may be in poor condition due to very heavy use, and these would be candidates for replacement. However, replacement of worn-out materials is dependent not only on current demand. More recent publications on a topic or the availability of newer editions, or both, should also be considered.

To keep the collection attractive and easy to browse, weeding (as deselection is commonly called) should also be done on a continual basis, although many librarians are reluctant to weed until they are unable to shelve any new books! Weeding increases the available space

TABLE 5.1 : Evaluation methods

User-Centered Evaluation	Advantages	Disadvantages
Circulation study	Easily counted, objective, probably available from automated circ system; flexibility in timing, sample size	Doesn't include in-house use or noncirculating collection; doesn't indicate user failures to find material (either available material or not available because of heavy use) or the impact of shelf placement
In-house use study	Gives a more complete picture when used with circ study; good for noncirculating collections	Affected by timing; materials in circulation can't be assessed for in-house use; does not indicate user failures to find material; difficult to control (patrons will reshelve in spite of signs)
User opinion survey	Permits direct feedback from users—and nonusers; can be simple (did you find what you were looking for today?) or complex	Expertise needed to construct a valid survey; users may be passive or uncooperative; users may not be aware of what library should/ can have/do; perceptions may not mirror use
Shelf-availability study	Reports failures; can be repeated to measure change	Needs the cooperation of users; doesn't reflect nonusers
ILL study	Easily counted; indication of patrons areas of interest	Doesn't count those who go directly to another library

Collection-Centered Evaluation	Advantages	Disadvantages
Checking lists, bibliographies	Easy to do; selector builds knowledge of the literature; gets the benefit of the expertise/ authority of the list compilers	List may have been used as a selection tool, or may not reflect library's purpose or users; there may not be an up-to-date list in some subjects
Looking over materials on the shelf	Quick; can apply to any library; can review for weeding, preservation, replacement at same time	Is evaluator knowledgeable? Produces no quantitative results. What about what's not on shelf?
Comparative statistics (age, growth rate, expenditures)	Easily collected; easy to compare	Stats from other libraries may have been recorded incorrectly or not comparable for some reason; labor intensive
Comparison to external standards	Using accepted standards may help build support—for example, funding agency wants library to meet standard, *but*	Funding agency may interpret minimum recommendation as sufficient or even maximum; similar types of libraries may have very different users, so one size standard doesn't fit all

---

Using Library Statistics to Understand and Evaluate Your Collection

Holdings, or Number of Items. Determine your total holdings as well as totals by format and genre for both adult and juvenile collections (such as nonfiction books, fiction books, audio materials, video materials, periodical subscriptions).

Circulation (Checkout) of Items. Collect circulation statistics to match the categories listed for holdings. You may also be able to have circulation statistics reported by Dewey number.

Number of Titles Added to the Collection Annually. It's useful to compare this figure to those for previous years at your library and for other libraries of comparable size. This figure is certainly affected by budget allocations, but also by price increases or the need to buy multiple copies of very popular titles.

Number of Items Discarded from the Collection. This information should be collected in the same categories as holdings to keep that information up-to-date.

Turnover Rate. Divide circulation by holdings. This number reflects the average number of times per year a collection has been checked out. If you have 40,000 items in your collections and had 80,000 circulations, the turnover rate is 2.

Vitality. What percentage of your collection is circulating? If those 80,000 circulations were of the same 5,000 items circulating 16 times per year (which is certainly possible if DVDs on one-week loan are a big part of your circulation), that means only one-eighth of your collection is circulating.

---

for newer, more appealing resources and removes the outdated, irrelevant, and unused. Think about whether retention of an item actually produces "negative value." Does it contain misinformation or obsolete information? Does it need special care for preservation or conservation that would take away from your acquisition budget? Is it in a format that is no longer used?

The acronym MUSTIE is often used to describe weeding criteria. Weed books that are

Misleading or factually inaccurate or both

Ugly (worn out beyond mending or rebinding)

Superseded by a new edition or a better source

Trivial (of no discernible literary or scientific merit)

Irrelevant to the needs and interests of your community

Elsewhere (the material may be easily borrowed from another source)

Just as with selection, you may want to establish criteria for deselection. The data gathered in collection evaluation will be helpful here. Material that has not circulated in two to five years and does not have in-house use may well be irrelevant to community interests or may just look so outdated that it will not catch a browser's eye. If shelves are really overcrowded, this alone will reduce circulation, as it becomes difficult to pull items out for browsing. Some of these items may begin to circulate if they are given a second chance through a display or face-out shelving.

Weeding fiction presents some challenges, because regardless of circulation, it may be desirable to keep some classic titles. Some questions to ask about weeding fiction are: Is this novel still used occasionally or mentioned in lists such as books for the college-bound? Will

Sample Circulation Policy

Issuing Cards

All borrowers must be registered and must have a valid library card to borrow library materials. Patrons must fill out an application form to register for a new library card. The following statement will be printed on the registration form for the patron's information and acceptance:

I agree to be responsible for all items borrowed with the library card issued in my name, including items borrowed with it by others with or without my consent unless I have previously reported the loss of my card. I promise to abide by all library rules and policies, both present and future, and to give prompt notice of change of address or loss of library card. I understand that there will be charges for overdue, lost, damaged, and stolen library materials. I understand that the library provides access to a broad range of resources and that it is my responsibility to judge for myself and for my children or minor dependents what resources are appropriate for my/our personal use.

Signature _____

Identification with proof of current residence is required. A driver's license or student ID is preferred; however, any other official photo ID with a recent nonpersonal piece of mail showing current address may be acceptable. Applicants under 13 years of age must have a parent or guardian give his or her consent on the application form before a new card can be issued. This parental signature is not required for children who are renewing cards.

Lost or Forgotten Cards

If a patron loses his or her library card, he or she should notify the library as soon as possible and request a replacement. All patrons, adult and juvenile, are expected to bring their library cards with them if they intend to check out items. A patron who has forgotten a card may check out materials upon the presentation of a photo ID, for a one-time, temporary checkout.

Loan Periods

1. Books circulate for three weeks. Books may be renewed once if there is not a waiting list for the title.

2. Current issues of periodicals do not circulate. Back issues circulate for two weeks.

3. Audiobooks, music CDs, and language instruction CDs circulate for two weeks and may be renewed once if there is not a waiting list for the title.

4. DVDs and games circulate for one week and may not be renewed.

5. Interlibrary loans are due on the date indicated by the lending library.

6. Reference books do not circulate.

7. The director may change the loan period for materials that are temporarily in great demand, such as for student projects.

8. Borrowers may have up to seventy-five items on a card at any time, with a limit of ten DVDs and fifteen CDs.

Fines and Charges

There are no fines for overdue materials. A first notice is sent after the material is due. If the material is not returned within a designated period, a bill will be sent for the material with the cost of replacement of the material and a service charge for processing, cataloging, and postage. If materials are returned damaged to the extent that they are unsuitable for the collection, the patron must pay the replacement cost and service charge. A notice of these charges will be sent to the borrower. Patrons who have been sent a bill shall be denied borrowing privileges until those overdue materials are returned or paid for if lost or damaged or both. (Patrons who damage and pay for materials owned by the library will be allowed to have those materials once payment has been received.)

Confidentiality

As specified in State Statute _____, records of any library supported by public funds indicating the identity of any individual who borrows or uses the library's documents or other materials, resources, or services may not be disclosed except by court order or to persons acting within the scope of their duties in the administration of the library or library system or to persons authorized by the individual to inspect such records.

This public library adheres strictly to all sections of this statute regarding the protection of the confidentiality of its users.

this item circulate if added to a display? Is the author still writing? If weeding a title based on condition, can it be replaced with a new edition that will look more attractive? Is the book part of a series (and if so, does the library have the rest)? Series titles are often meant to be read in order so libraries often try to maintain the complete run. However, if the first title in the series circulates but not the rest of the series, consider weeding the others. And when deciding to weed or replace audiobooks or films, consider the format above all.

In many areas of the nonfiction collection, currency and accuracy are extremely important. Outdated items may continue to circulate if nothing newer is available, so some titles should be evaluated by their age and content. Table 5.2 offers suggestions on when to weed nonfiction based on Dewey subject categories.

Many libraries are reducing the size of the print reference collection as "ready reference" in many subject areas has moved online. Circulation data won't help with these weeding decisions, as reference items generally don't circulate, but keep the current and future use in mind. For example, items like city directories may eventually be useful for genealogical purposes, but they could be shelved elsewhere. Consider the currency of the reference works (dictionaries and atlases should be replaced as new editions become available), whether patrons have shown any interest in older holdings, and the physical condition of the material. Are some things sacred, to be kept regardless of use? Local history materials and local authors might fall into this category. If the local public library doesn't keep these items, who will? However, if materials are fragile and require conservation and storage conditions that cannot be provided by the public library, it might be prudent to transfer these holdings to a local or state historical society.

Once items have been identified for withdrawal from the collection, they can be sorted into three categories.

1. Keep, but repair. (Think about whether it would be cheaper to replace, or if there is a newer edition. Ask yourself one last time, do we need this?)

TABLE 5.2 : Weeding nonfiction by Dewey number

Subject	When to weed	Special considerations
000—General/Computer info	Computer info outdated in 3 years	
100—Philosophy and psychology	"Pop" psychology or gimmicky titles outdated in 2–3 years	
200—Religion	Keep current as there is usually a high turnover rate	Does the religion collection reflect your community?
300—Social sciences	Law, government, and topics used in school reports must be up-to-date	Watch balance of controversial topics
400—Languages	May have heavy use in English-language-learning programs; check condition	Replace as necessary based on community needs
500—Pure sciences	Retain basic historical works but continuously replace outdated works	
600—Applied sciences	Health/medical books change rapidly, many outdated in 3 years	Consider danger of misinformation on shelves; keep all collector and repair books unless hobbyists are now using online sources
700—Arts and recreation	Evaluate for accuracy, styles; many can be kept until worn out	
800—Literature	Keep most recent editions	Get reading lists from local high schools
900—History/travel/biography	Travel guidebooks outdated in 2 years; biography—stay current with popular figures	Evaluate history books for demand, accuracy, relationship to current events; consider the age group reading biographies

2. Replace with new copy.

3. Remove from building and from catalog. These are materials that might go into a fund-raising book sale, be given to another organization, or be destroyed.

It is common to worry that the item discarded today will be requested tomorrow or that you are discarding the last copy of an old book. It can be very reassuring to look up an item in WorldCat (www.worldcat.org) to see if there are other copies in your area. Some patrons (and staff, too) get emotional about throwing books away. Examples of materials that need to be weeded are very helpful. Save the most blatant examples of materials that have "negative value" to show to anyone who complains about the removal of old materials.

What is the difference between preservation and conservation? *Preservation* maintains the access to the intellectual content; *conservation* maintains the artifact. The goal of the collection review is to ensure that materials significant to the collection remain available to the library's users. In the small public library this primarily means finding ways to extend the useful shelf life of the collection, rather than conserving it for the future. Materials in need of preservation can be identified following use or through a collection survey or systematic shelf review and can be ranked according to *importance* (highest use, important local collections), *risk* (brittle paper/newsprint, heavy use), and *feasibility* (affordable, repairable in-house). Materials of lesser importance requiring expensive repair can be left alone as "planned deterioration." Items that are not rare or especially valuable can be handled with temporary repair measures to keep them in circulation. This stop-gap is done for items that will eventually be weeded.

For items of value, their rarity, their provenance (how they came to be part of this collection), and their significance to the community must also be considered. If the value is in the artifact, rather than just in the information within, the skills of a trained conservator may be needed to ensure the item's survival and continued availability for use, while maintaining its physical form. If the artifact is less important, other options might include acquiring a reprint or another edition, making a preservation photocopy, or purchasing or producing a microform edition (often used for newspapers). Digitizing is not considered a true preservation method, because file formats and digital storage media can change, but digitizing unique materials does help preserve them because they can be handled less often.

If you routinely find material in poor condition, the causes should be examined. The most common problems are climate control (temperature, humidity, light), biological factors (insects, mold, mildew), and people! Poor handling of books and other materials by users (and even by staff) is one of the greatest threats to their condition. Staff should be trained on proper handling and shelving of materials, and patrons may need gentle reminders such as signs on the book drop that caution against putting wet materials inside. Finally, if there is recurring mutilation of certain items, decide whether such items will be replaced and consider the need for secure shelving.

CHALLENGES TO LIBRARY MATERIALS

In the Library Bill of Rights, the American Library Association affirms that all libraries are forums for information and ideas and that the following basic policies should guide their services.

> Books and other library resources should be provided for the interest, information, and enlightenment of all people of the community the library serves. Materials should not be excluded because of the origin, background, or views of those contributing to their creation.

> Libraries should provide materials and information presenting all points of view on current and historical issues. Materials should not be proscribed or removed because of partisan or doctrinal disapproval.

Libraries should challenge censorship in the fulfillment of their responsibility to provide information and enlightenment.

Libraries should cooperate with all persons and groups concerned with resisting abridgment of free expression and free access to ideas.

The library's collection development policy forms the basis of any response to a materials challenge and should cover what and why you own and acquire what you do. In fact, maintaining a materials selection policy is often the first step in dealing with any challenge, as it can be shown to anyone who asks why the library will or won't acquire a particular title. There should be a clearly defined method for handling complaints.

It is important to listen calmly and courteously to any complaints about materials. Explain the Library Bill of Rights. Many complaints have to do with children's materials and can be deflected simply by pointing out that the collection must serve a wide age range and that parents are encouraged to help their children choose age-appropriate materials. However, the response may be, "It's not my child I'm concerned about." Others who challenge materials may find some views so objectionable that they want to keep others from reading or seeing the

---

Citizen Request for Reconsideration of Library Materials

Author _____

Title _____

Book _____ Periodical _____ Other _____ Publisher/Date _____

Please state the reason for your request: _____
_____

Have you read/viewed/listened to this work/exhibition in its entirety?
_____

What are the positive points of this material? _____
_____

What would you like the library to do about this work? _____
_____

Is there another work you would recommend on this subject?
_____
_____

Have you read the library's Collection Development Policy? Yes _____ No _____

Request initiated by _____

Address _____

State _____ Zip _____ Phone _____

Do you represent:

_____ Yourself

_____ Organization (name) _____

Date: _____ Signature of Patron: _____

Date: _____ Received by Staff Member: _____

TALES FROM THE FIELD: Censorship or Prudent Selection?

My previous position was in a very conservative town, purchasing for a very conservative public. Even many of my best volunteers were questioners of materials. I do struggle with self-censorship, and with a limited budget as an excuse, it is pretty easy to fall into this trap. So while I do agree with staying away from labeling and censoring and separating materials based on content (other than children/YA/adult), I will be perfectly honest and say from time to time I needed to remind myself of intellectual freedom because of the local pressure I would get.

A good question for me when I choose not to purchase then is this: Am I not purchasing because I know it will be controversial, or am I not purchasing because it's not going to circulate well? Is this material going to help balance out my collection?

Source: Nicole Overbeck, Library Director, Wautoma (Wisconsin) Library.

---

work. These are challenges that should be made in writing, and the patron should be given a form to request reconsideration of library materials.

When a written challenge is received, the library board should be notified. The board should create an appropriate team of reviewers to consider the request. Although there's often no need to rush through the process, the library still should proceed diligently and prepare a thoughtful response to the complainant. Materials acquired in keeping with the library's selection criteria will rarely be removed completely, but it is possible that the patron has identified something that would be more suitably shelved with adult materials rather than in the children's section.

NOTES

1. Lionel McColvin, *The Theory of Book Selection for Public Libraries* (London: Grafton, 1925).
2. Francis Drury, *Book Selection* (Chicago: American Library Association, 1930).
3. Helen Haines, *Living with Books: The Art of Book Selection* (New York: Columbia University Press, 1935).
4. Robert Broadus, *Selecting Materials for Libraries,* 2nd edition (New York: H. W. Wilson, 1981).

CHAPTER SIX

SERVICES AND PROGRAMS

IDENTIFYING THE PROPER SERVICE MIX

Chapter 1 of this book, "Who Do You Work For?" provides an overall view of strategic planning on the topics of service roles and responses, the planning time line, basic elements of the planning document, and collecting data.

The service roles and responses address three general areas of planning: what the library does, who the library serves, and the resources required to meets its goals.[1] The selection and prioritization of these elements of the planning process require input from community stakeholders: the public, local elected and appointed officials, the business community, service groups, and civic organizations. The services and programs a library chooses to offer must consider the need to build a common agenda and to achieve mutually overlapping goals. As shown in table 6.1, a series of surveys conducted in 1993 illustrates a gulf between how librarians and the public perceive the importance of various service roles.[2]

One of the primary challenges of the planning process is to select and prioritize the services that best fit the needs of the community. As we move into an era of increasingly limited resources, it becomes even more counterproductive for a library to attempt to be all things to all people.

The introductory chapter ("Why Plan?") of *Planning for Results, the Guidebook: A Public Library Transformation Process* notes that "[m]any libraries try to do too many things and end up doing many things inadequately instead of doing a few things well."[3] A successful planning process focuses on three areas of general review:

- services and programs the library should provide
- services and programs the library should not provide
- how resources are allocated among the services and programs the library provides

TABLE 6.1 : Prioritizing public library service roles

Libraries' primary and secondary goal areas	% selected	Survey of 1,001 members of public and 300 opinion leaders	% selected
Popular Materials Center	**94**	Formal Education Support Center	88
Preschoolers' Door to Learning	78	Independent Learning Center	85
Reference Library	78	Preschoolers' Door to Learning	83
		Research Library	68
		Community Information Center	66
		Community Activities Center	52
		Popular Materials Center	**51**

Source: Annabel K. Stephens, *Assessing the Public Library Planning Process* (New York: Ablex Publishing, 1995).

In *Administration of the Small Public Library,* Darlene E. Weingand asks the question, "What are the library's products?"[4] To provide the answer, she references Philip Kotler's *Marketing for Nonprofit Organizations* and provides the following terminology and definitions.

Product mix: the set of all product lines and items that a particular organization makes available to its customers

Product line: a group of products within a product mix that are closely related, either because they function in a similar manner, are made available to the same customers, or are marketed through the same types of outlets

Product item: a distinct unit within a product line that is distinguishable by size, appearance, price, or some other attribute[5]

SETTING PRIORITIES

One way to set priorities, particularly if you are reexamining your library's service program in light of budget adjustments or new initiatives, is to evaluate the relationship between cost and demand. Take a look at your current product mix and ask yourself the following questions:

- What is the cost of this service? (staff, materials, equipment, furnishings, other operating expenditures)

PRODUCT MIX: Services

This text box is the first of a series of three that contain menus of service and program options. No small library, of course, will have the resources to accomplish all of them. Selection and prioritization of a product mix will be reflected in the library's strategic plan. And the lists, of course, are not meant to be comprehensive.

Circulation
- Online public access catalog
- Holds (patron-initiated requests from other libraries)
- Staff-assisted checkout, payment of fines/fees
- Self-service (checkout, holds pick-up, payment of fines/fees)

Public Service (Children, Teens, Adults)
- Collections of print and audiovisual materials
- Special displays
- Programs designed to meet a variety of informational and recreational needs
- Bibliographies

Reference (for all ages)
- Answering questions/providing assistance

In-library

Telephone

E-mail

Instant Messaging/Chat
- Readers' advisory/family literacy
- Interlibrary loan
- Homework help center
- Jobs and career information/small business resource center
- Specialized collections

Local history

Yearbooks

Clippings, pamphlet file

Digital resources

Public Access Computers
- Internet
- E-mail
- Office applications (word processing, spreadsheets, etc.)

Outreach
- Deposit collections in nursing homes, day care centers, etc.
- Homebound/books-by-mail service
- Special needs: hearing loss, low vision
- School visits/Booktalks
- Jail service
- Bookmobile

PRODUCT MIX: Programs

This is the second of a series of three text boxes that contain menus of service and program options. No small library, of course, will have the resources to accomplish all of them. Selection and prioritization of a product mix will be reflected in the library's strategic plan. And the lists, of course, are not designed to be comprehensive.

All Ages
- Summer/winter reading programs
- Author visits
- Book group discussions
- Film series
- Music
- General interest topics

Adults
- Job search skills/career information
- Computer instruction

Formal Group

Informal One-on-One
- Travel/Nature
- Cooking demonstrations (where space, equipment, and fire codes permit)
- History and reminiscing (sharing life stories)

Teens
- Gaming
- Advisory committee
- Writing and art contests
- Video production
- Shared development of website
- Book and movie release parties
- Special interests: tie-dye, mehndi

Children
- Storytimes (lapsit, toddler, preschool, all ages, bilingual, etc.)
- Crafts
- "Books to Cooks"
- Reading to dogs
- Holiday-themed activities
- Sleepovers
- "Instant Theater"
- Play groups
- Specific audiences: homeschoolers, school class, and preschool visits

PRODUCT MIX: Other Amenities

The third of a series of three text boxes that contain menus of service and program options. No small library, of course, will have the resources to accomplish all of them. Selection and prioritization of a product mix will be reflected in the library's strategic plan. And the lists, of course, are not designed to be comprehensive.

Equipment
- Public access computers
- Laptops (generally for in-library use)
- Photocopiers (black and white, color, two-sided)
- Fax machine
- Energy meters
- Video game gear
- Still and digital video cameras
- Public address system

Gathering Space
- Community meeting room (with kitchen facilities)
- Study rooms for individual and small group use

Promotion
- Newsletter (print and/or online)
- Flyers that promote specific programs and services
- Use of local media: community access cable TV, television stations in your library's service area market, radio, newspapers, weekly shoppers
- Facebook
- Twitter
- Flickr
- Blogs

Display Space
- Bulletin board
- Secure, enclosed display case for use by community groups
- Exhibit space for artwork
- "Giveaway" shelves (e.g., magazine exchange)

Friends Book Sales
- Dedicated space versus temporary location
- Ongoing and/or scheduled

Merchandise
- Book bags
- T-shirts/caps
- Posters
- Notecards/postcards

Food and Beverages
- Café
- Coffee bar

- How much demand is there for this service?
- Over the past five years, has demand increased, decreased, or remained the same?

The relationship between cost and demand is best determined by using the following guidelines.[6] Each example includes a series of hypothetical statements that are likely to arise during staff and board discussions.

High Cost/High Demand. Materials and services for which there is significant demand and that are expensive to maintain. They need to be carefully evaluated on an annual basis.

Example: Preschool Storytimes

- In general, wage and fringe benefits expenditures comprise between 65 percent and 70 percent of a library's annual budget. And, in order to be successful in this area, there is no getting around the staff time spent on planning, promotion, and implementation.
- Surveys have confirmed that public library services to children and young adults should occupy a high priority in the service plan of every public library because they build the base of future users.[7]

Example: Audiobooks

- Cost per unabridged title is generally in the $50–$100 range.
- Collection has a high turnover rate (number of circulations per title on an annual basis).
- Patrons use a shared online catalog to request titles but have made it clear they want the library to have a browsing collection.

High Cost/Low Demand. Materials and services for which there is negligible demand and that are expensive to maintain. Serious consideration should be given to phasing them out.

Example: Print Reference Collection

- Standard reference titles such as encyclopedias, handbooks, and directories require regular and costly updates.
- As use of full-text online databases has increased, the use of print resources has decreased.
- Many libraries have already downsized their print reference collections with hardly a peep of protest.

Low Cost/High Demand. Materials and services for which there is significant demand and that are relatively inexpensive to maintain.

Example: Bulletin Board/Display Space

- Information about community events and organizations is given prominent display just inside the main entrance to the library, which results in high visibility and interest.
- An increasingly popular magazine exchange was initiated within the past two years.
- Organization and maintenance are assigned to a volunteer under the supervision of a staff person.

Low Cost/Low Demand. Materials and services for which there is negligible demand and that are relatively inexpensive to maintain. Decisions need to be made on a case-by-case basis, keeping in mind that some of these items or services may have a high, perhaps overlooked, public-relations value.

Example: Public Access Typewriter

- Most patrons have made the transition to using word processing programs.
- The one typewriter the library owns is nearly twenty years old; the only person available to service it has indicated he is likely to give up that portion of his repair business.
- A review of the reservation log sheet indicates that the typewriter is used on average once per week.

Example: Art Reproductions

- The collection has been in place for more than thirty years, but no new items have been purchased for or otherwise added to it for the past decade.
- The fifty items circulate an average of less than two times per year.
- The space in which the items are displayed could be better used for an expansion of the library's public access computers.

An ongoing review of library services and programs ensures that staff make the best and most efficient use of available resources. Vigilance is highly recommended. The regular introduction of new products and formats, for example, requires a series of carefully considered collection development decisions. Since 1980, most public libraries have added (and, in some cases, subsequently removed) an array of new formats to their shelves, including music audio cassettes, books on cassette, book/cassette kits, board books, CD-ROM software, music compact discs, books on CD, DVDs, video games, and digital audiobooks.

This proliferation begs the question: How much variety can libraries afford? The answer will vary from location to location, but in general it boils down to this: As much as your available space and resources allow.

EVALUATING SERVICES AND PROGRAMS —————————

A SWOT analysis is an environmental scanning process that allows an organization to conduct an internal analysis of its strengths (S) and weaknesses (W) and an external analysis of opportunities (O) and threats (T). As a tool that allows libraries to both plan for and evaluate services and programs, a SWOT analysis serves a dual purpose. Initially, it provides a planning team a structured activity to assess various aspects of the goals and objectives it hopes to achieve within the service roles or responses it has chosen to emphasize. As a follow-up, it offers staff and board members a clear-cut method to determine where progress has been made (or why progress was hindered) and to fine-tune the library's strategies.

The four elements of a SWOT analysis are defined as follows:

Strengths. Internal attributes of the organization (e.g., budget, staff, collections, facilities, access, public relations) that are helpful in achieving the objective.

Weaknesses. Internal attributes of the organization that are harmful to achieving the objective.

Opportunities. External conditions (e.g., political, economic, social, technological) that are helpful in achieving the objective.

Threats. External conditions that could do damage to the organization's performance.

Here's a hypothetical example of how a SWOT analysis can be used to assess a reference services program.

Strengths

- affordable access to high-quality, online, full-text databases through a state consortium
- a comfortably furnished, well-designed service area, with a central desk and sufficient computer stations

Weaknesses

- inconsistent staff skill levels in conducting an effective reference interview and finding information online
- insufficient bandwidth; slow response time for online searches

Opportunities

- a network of retired librarians who are willing to provide small-group or individual training sessions for staff
- federal funds to bring fiber optics and greatly increased bandwidth to all public libraries in the state

Threats

- proposed cuts in state funding that threaten to severely reduce the amount of funding available for statewide databases
- the question that has been with us since the mid-1990s: why do we need libraries when we have the Internet?

Once the environmental scan is completed—and the preceding example would be just a small element of it—the final step of the SWOT analysis is to ask a series of questions about the library's priorities.

- What strengths do we focus on? What services and programs should we enhance?
- What weaknesses do we work to minimize? What services and programs should we deemphasize or cut?
- What opportunities should we work to our advantage? What strategies are necessary to achieve this?
- What are the most serious threats to reaching our goals? What strategies are necessary to neutralize them?

The ability to make steady, measurable progress in achieving service and program goals requires a careful attention to detail and a clear understanding of both the internal and external environments in which a library operates.

The following sections of this chapter provide an overview of a typical library service mix. They provide some underpinnings of a philosophy of service and describe suggested activities. We particularly appreciate the thoughtful perspectives provided by our "Tales from the Field" contributors.

YOUTH SERVICES

A classic article, one that still deserves to be required reading for all library directors, provides some useful advice for developing and prioritizing library services. In "Creating the Library Habit," Barbara Will Razzano summarizes the findings of a series of studies on library use.[8]

- People who use the library as children are more likely to use it as adults.
- People who use the library as children are more likely to have children who are library users.

Razzano refers to the second finding as a "pyramid effect," one that ties directly to the title of her article and leads her to offer the following recommendation:

> Because they build the base of future users, public library services to children and young adults should occupy a high priority in the service plan of every public library. The overwhelming majority of all current adult library users began that use while under the age of 18.[9]

One of the greatest challenges for librarians who serve youth is to provide services and programs to a general user group that spans a range of eighteen years—from lapsit storytimes and board books for children as young as six months to gaming activities and graphic novels for teens. Like a moving target, the needs and interests of youth vary greatly as they progress through the first five stages of life: infancy, toddler, preschool, childhood, and adolescence.

Many children's librarians have increasingly emphasized the family aspect of youth services by rethinking what type of seating is provided and how collections are displayed. Instead of offering only furnishings of a size designed for children, the youth area includes a variety of comfortable seating for adults, encouraging them to remain nearby while a child is browsing for books or attending a storytime. Libraries have also added computer stations that comfortably accommodate a parent and child working together. In addition, permanent collections of parenting materials or other appropriate subject matter, in both print and audiovisual formats, are now shelved in the same area as picture books and easy readers for the sake of convenience and easy access.

The services and program choices available to youth librarians are limitless, but it is not within the scope of this book to provide a detailed and comprehensive overview of the possibilities. For this reason, we offer you a series of "Tales from the Field."

The first tale presents general suggestions for creating memorable programs and offers a few specific examples.

The second tale is an effective promotional piece for a library's summer reading program, with special attention given to the importance of preventing "achievement loss" and setting aside specific times to read during the day.

The third tale provides straightforward and clear-eyed advice on how to make your library a welcoming place for teens.

ADULT SERVICES

According to statistics published by the Institute for Museum and Library Services, nearly 3.5 million people attended library-initiated programs during 2008. Attendance at adult programs accounts for slightly less than 25 percent of this total, although this figure represents an increase from 19 percent in 2004, the first year for which these statistics were collected at the national level. Clearly, public libraries place a strong emphasis on offering storytimes and other programs to children, but the numbers indicate an increased emphasis on programs for adults.

Even on a small scale, adult programming provides a host of benefits. A regular series of programs helps to expand the library's role as a community resource. Adult programs provide opportunities for lifelong learning, are likely to attract nonusers to the library, and enhance the library's visibility. Ideally, they include a broad spectrum of topics and a variety of viewpoints. At the same time, staff responsible for program planning and implementation need to select program ideas that are relevant to the interests and issues of the community they serve.

Library-initiated programs generally fall into three broad categories. The first category utilizes library staff and in-house resources exclusively, as is sometimes accomplished in the development of basic computer classes. On a much different note, the Lester Public Library in

TALES FROM THE FIELD: Successful Programs for Kids

How do you create successful programs for kids beyond your storytimes? It's an ear-to-the-ground thing: ask kids and people who work with them what is currently hot; subscribe to electronic discussion lists like Pubyac (www.pubyac.org) and RSS feeds of blogs that share program ideas; and take advantage of movies and pop culture to create programs that resonate with kids.

You don't need much money or many staffers to create memorable programs, just:

- enthusiasm and looking at ways to highlight your collections through creative programs (games, science, literary characters, vehicles, poetry, origami, crafts, dinosaurs, and more)
- ability to reach out, network, and partner within your community and schools to discover people willing to share skills, talents, and ideas for your programs
- willingness to change, adapt, evolve, and play to make programs fun for kids and families
- realization that programs may be more than in-house events—they might reach out to partner with schools for mutual school-year reading programs; or be a "Free-quent Reader" type club card that encourages using the library often; or more visits to schools during the school year to promote reading, books, and library use

Consider offering these surefire hits at your library:

Stuffed Animal Sleepover. Share a few stories with kids and critters, then tuck the animals in and ask the children to kiss them goodbye. After the children leave, pose their fuzzy lovables near books, in the book drop, answering the phone, and listening to stories. Print a few photos and give to the kids the next day when they pick up their stuffed friends.

Book Parties. Throw a party tied to a literary character when book-based movies debut or a new edition of a popular series is published. Make up a few trivia questions, read from the book, and play one or two fun games (based on traditional children's games) themed to the character.

Vehicle Petting Zoo. Arrange for trucks, motorcycles, heavy equipment, and police and fire vehicles to park in the library lot and let kids get up close and personal.

Instant Theater. Chose a favorite picture book (*The Very Hungry Caterpillar, Where the Wild Things Are, Anansi and the Moss Covered Rock,* etc.). The practice and play happen all in the same hour. Read the book, share basic stage directions (always face the audience, be quiet when offstage), and practice. You narrate and the kids follow simple directions. Families become the audience for the under-five-minute play and, at the end, a cast party, of course, with treats and where the young stars shine!

Source: Marge Loch-Wouters, Youth Services Coordinator, La Crosse (Wisconsin) Public Library.

Two Rivers, Wisconsin, a community with an aging demographic, has achieved a great measure of success with its Story Circles, a regularly scheduled series of group discussions that provide participants an opportunity to reminisce and share their life experiences on such topics as the Great Depression, medical assistance, and birth. The most common example of the in-house program, however, is the book discussion group, which dovetails perfectly with the library's traditional mission. Retired librarian Lisa Cihlar provides some useful firsthand advice on developing successful strategies in this specific area of programming.

TALES FROM THE FIELD: How to Conduct an Effective Book Group

Book groups can be a wonderful way to get to know your public and create goodwill for the library. I ran book groups in every public library I worked for and made some lifelong friends in the process.

Here are some things I learned.

Have a sense of humor. If you can laugh at yourself and admit that you forgot to order the multiple copies of books in time, but they will be in within a few days, people won't get mad. If you pick a book that everyone hates, laugh it off and have a huge discussion as to why it was so horrible and what would have made it a better read and whether there were any redeeming qualities at all.

Use name tags. People like to be addressed by their names; it makes them feel part of the group. Get everyone to talk. I always like to do an around-the-room at the start and finish of every meeting to give the people who are more reticent a chance to talk. But if some people want to pass, don't push it.

As for the person who takes over, it's best to confront this early and as often as it takes to keep the discussion open to all. *"Mary, it is interesting that you learned so much on your trip to London, but to get back to the book, Jane, what did you think about it?"* Do this as often as necessary. Try to steer rather than rule the group.

Finally, I always told my groups that I was running a friendly dictatorship. I would chose a wide selection of books and let the group vote on the choices, but they were my choices based on the number of copies I could get and on books that I was fairly sure would be good for discussion, and (here's where the dictator part comes in) books that I was sure I could read and discuss intelligently.

Source: Lisa Cihlar, retired library director.

More typically, the library seeks out other community resources to share in the development and sponsorship of programs. In this second category, the library actively partners with other groups and organizations as well as educational and cultural institutions, tapping into their specialized or unique expertise in order to ensure its programming offers a broad spectrum of topics. Many of these agencies are willing to participate at no cost or for a nominal fee. In some cases, individuals with no particular affiliation, such as collectors or hobbyists, are asked to develop and present programs. Where funding and space permit, professional performers—local musicians, for example—add a lively note to a library's program schedule.

The third category combines elements of programming and outreach. Adult literacy and English as a New Language programs, to use two related examples, fit naturally with the public library's mission of meeting educational and informational needs and its role of being a resource for lifelong learning. Working with local agencies, libraries can assist in the recruitment of volunteers and offer meeting room space for training and tutoring. In addition, many libraries, often under the guidance of a library system or other consortium, develop and maintain appropriate collections to support literacy and language programs.

REFERENCE SERVICES

One of the most discussed technological impacts on libraries is the decreased number of reference questions answered by staff since the Internet became generally available. According

Get ready . . . it's coming . . . summer vacation! Long, warm days mean lots of time spent outside digging in the garden, swimming, and playing sports. My children spend every moment outside that they can, and I'm sure yours are no different. This summer, let's all exercise our brains just a little, too. Take a few minutes to wind down before bed by reading.

Have your children start out the day by reading during breakfast before heading out to the pool. On a rainy day, taking an hour to read a good book will keep boredom away. Children love to pick out their own books, and summer provides a great opportunity for children to read for pleasure. Better yet, make reading a part of your day in order to set an excellent example for your children about the importance of reading.

As you embark on sun, fun, and relaxation, who wants to think about school? I certainly don't! But just a few minutes a day spent reading during the summer months can make a world of difference to a child's success next year. Numerous studies have shown that reading over break prevents "summer reading loss." This loss is cumulative, which means that children don't catch up each fall after spending a summer without a book. This deficit can mean falling behind their classmates in reading skills. By the end of sixth grade, children who lose reading skills each summer can end up as much as two years behind their classmates.

A 2007 study published in *American Sociological Review* reveals that the achievement gaps among students in ninth grade can be traced back to the loss in reading skills occurring over the summer months throughout elementary school. This study also provides evidence that summer loss can shape achievement in grade nine and beyond, suggesting it may be indicative of the separation between college-track students and non-college-track students.

Now that you are worried about your child's progress and future: *relax*. The solution is simple: reading for pleasure as little as fifteen minutes a day, or five books a summer, can change this course. At the library, we all want to help your children find books they will want to read. Make this a stress-free summer—help your child to explore reading for fun. This can make your job easier and your child's life more satisfying.

Motivation seems to be a regular, ongoing problem that many parents struggle with when it comes to persuading their children to read. The free Summer Reading Program (SRP) at your library can have a significant impact on children's reading skills while providing motivational incentives. Nontraditional materials can help motivate even the most reluctant of readers. By returning to the library every year for the reading program, you can build reading into your child's summer routine.

Source: Kirsten Mortimer, Youth Services Associate, Pauline Haass Public Library, Sussex, Wisconsin.

to annual Wisconsin Public Library Service Data statistics, for example, these numbers have experienced a significant and steady statewide decline since the late 1990s.

- 5,773,435 questions answered in 1999
- 5,260,932 in 2004, a decrease of nearly 9 percent
- 4,623,686 in 2009, a five-year decrease of 12 percent and a ten-year decrease of 20 percent

Although not strictly an apples-to-apples comparison, statistics collected by the Institute of Museum and Library Services show a decrease in the number of reference questions asked per capita, from 1.08 in 2003 to 1.00 in 2008, or an estimated decrease of 14 million questions.[10]

TALES FROM THE FIELD:
Dos and Don'ts of Building Effective Teen Services

Do . . .
Look at teen developmental needs and at what teens consider to be their needs:
- Brainstorm how the library could meet those needs.
- Offer volunteer opportunities.

Create a welcoming teen space:
- Let teens have input and help with artistic endeavors.

Start a Teen Advisory Committee:
- Let teens know you value their opinion.
- They will feel invested in the library.
- Your circ will go up as you purchase the materials that teens want to see.
- Your program attendance will increase as they choose the programs.

Look at what others are doing to serve teens:
- In your community (youth center/schools) so as not to duplicate
- Teen websites from other libraries (great places for ideas)
- Electronic discussion lists (great ideas and advice)
- Bookstores (how do they market to teens?)

Try to raise support for Teen Services:
- With your library director, library board, other staff, and community

Protect yourself in case of intellectual freedom challenges:
- Work with other staff to create an effective collection development policy.
- Research and practice how you would respond to a challenge.

Perform outreach:
- Write teachers to offer booktalks and tours; mention upcoming programs.
- Talk with school librarians about coordinating efforts.
- Look into other community organizations you could partner with.

Pursue publicity:
- Put notices in newspapers, newsletters, and posters around town.
- Brainstorm with your teen group to find hot spots to hang publicity.
- Keep current with popular media and technology that teens enjoy to understand changing trends.

Don't . . .
Try too hard to be hip and cool:
- Teens are uncomfortable when you try to be someone you're not.
- They need someone who will set rules and enforce them and who will earn their respect, even if they groan about it.

Be condescending or preachy:
- Treat teens with as much respect as adults, and they will respect you in return.

Have an outdated collection:
- Weed regularly.

Get discouraged:
- It takes time for program attendance to grow and for teens to know that you are their advocate.

Source: Rebecca Van Dan, Middleton (Wisconsin) Public Library.

In spite of this decline, Internet access as an element of reference services continues to demonstrate strong growth as a service provided by public libraries. At the same time, the proliferation of computer technology and its enthusiastic embrace by much of the public has greatly changed the way in which library staff plan for and provide services. According to statistics collected by the National Center for Education Statistics (NCES), slightly more than 95 percent of U.S. public libraries already offered public access to the Internet in 2000, just a few years after this service began to be available on a widespread basis. (The percentage was considerably lower in libraries with a service population under 1,000.) The total number of Internet computers available for public use at this time was just under 100,000.[11]

In just seven years, the number of public access computers in libraries more than doubled. As an indication of how popular this activity has become, these 200,000+ computers were used 357,000,000 times to access such services as searching online databases, placing holds, looking for information on the World Wide Web, using online databases, using e-mail, filling out online applications and other documents, scanning photos, and much more. In public libraries with a service population of less than 10,000, the average annual number of uses ranges from 1,520 (population less than 1,000) to 14,636 (population 5,000–9,999).[12] It is not unreasonable to assume that a substantial number of these uses are going to generate requests for staff assistance.

In light of this rapidly growing use of public access computers, what are the service implications for libraries?

Here's a real-life example.

In a presentation to their county board of supervisors, six directors of rural public libraries, all of them located in communities of less than 2,000 population, described how Wi-Fi use by job seekers is their number one growth area in service. The staff at these libraries increasingly find themselves providing assistance in writing résumés and cover letters, proofreading job application materials, accessing online job listings, and locating maps and directions for job fairs and job interviews. In many communities, the public library has become the de facto job center.

Suggested Cosponsors for Library Program Development

University extension services
- Gardening and landscaping
- Family financial management
- Small business assistance

Arts and cultural organizations
- Art
- Music
- Poetry
- Theater

Public health agencies
- Diet and nutrition
- Wellness
- Exercise/yoga
- Preventive health care
- Aging/Caregiving

Historical societies (stories of notable people and places)
- Local
- County
- State

Genealogical society
- Research methods
- Available resources

As anyone who works at a public service desk will attest, the use of computers in libraries generates ongoing requests for assistance. Often, these requests require staff to move away from the desk in order to understand the patron's need and to respond effectively. As a result, this type of assistance is likely to involve elements of formal and informal instruction. In the small public library, providing quick answers to directional or ready-reference questions is no longer the norm.

READERS' ADVISORY

> You find out what books the actual users of the library need, and your judgment improves in regard to the kind of books it is best to add to it. You see what subjects the constituency of the institution are interested in, and what is the degree of simplicity they require in the presentation of knowledge.[13]

Samuel Swett Green, generally considered to be the "father of reference work," shared this somewhat florid definition of readers' advisory service in an article written for *American Library Journal*. In it, he set forth four general goals for reference librarians, one of them being "helping people select good reading material." So begins the first of four periods that Bill Crowley limns in a 2005 *Public Libraries* article, "Rediscovering the History of Readers Advisory Service."[14]

- 1876 to 1920—Inventing readers' advisory
- 1920 to 1940—Privileging *nonfiction* readers' advisory
- 1940 to 1984—Readers' advisory "lost" in adult services
- 1984 to date—Reviving readers' advisory

The spark for this revival took place in 1982 with the publication of *Genreflecting: A Guide to Reading Interests in Popular Fiction.* Now in its sixth edition (2006), *Genreflecting* covers the popular genres of crime, adventure, romance, science fiction, fantasy, and horror; describes the numerous subgenres within each general category; and provides lists of recommended books in each category. In other words, it follows Green's advice about "helping people select good reading material." *Genreflecting* kick-started a small industry of similar publications (*What Do I Read Next?*; *Sequels: An Annotated Guide to Novels in Series*) and, within twenty years, brought about an abundance of readers' advisory websites and blogs, including, perhaps most famously, readers' advisory icon Nancy Pearl's *Book Lust.*

What does it take to become a skilled readers' advisor? Being an enthusiastic and voracious reader certainly provides a distinct advantage. The best starting point, however, is to develop a personal reading program, one that includes books that fall outside your general areas of interest. Read widely and indiscriminately, in other words, and develop "sound-bite" summaries to help you remember main characters and key elements of the storyline.

In addition, it's important to keep track of publishing trends and what types of books your patrons are likely to request. Familiarize yourself with books in series, a very popular format with readers. Learn about authors who are creating a buzz, as they are likely to become popular choices with book discussion groups. Discover what people are eager to read by checking the number of holds on new or soon-to-be-published books in your online catalog. Become a regular reader of book reviews, both in the traditional media and online. Most importantly, know where to find information about books and authors in a variety of formats. Organize links to the best websites and blogs on your library's website.

Library staff who provide readers' advisory service may discover that their advice is requested away from the library. How often have you heard this response after describing what you do for a living? "You work in a library? I need to know a good book to read."

TECHNOLOGY AND LIBRARY SERVICE

Although it's possible to encounter only one major building or remodeling project during the course of a career, a library director faces the ongoing challenge of reallocating space to ensure the optimum use of floor area for the library's menu of services. In many small libraries, particularly where space for existing services is already at a premium, even the addition of just one computer workstation is not likely to take place until it is determined which part of a collection or what section of seating space will be eliminated or placed in storage. Library planning consultant Anders Dahlgren recommends that anywhere from 35 to 50 square feet of space be allocated for each public access computer station.[15] In other words, a final decision may require eliminating as many as 650 books in order to add one new computer.

In addressing the service implications of computers and technology, libraries have learned that a one-size-fits-all approach is not the most effective way to meet their patrons' wide-ranging

---

How to Read a Book in Ten Minutes

It's a cliché, but judge the book by its cover.

- The cover may be a key decision maker for a person browsing the new-book display.
- Covers are designed to encourage impulse purchases—or checkouts, from the library's perspective.

Read the blurb.

- It's what the publisher wants you to know about the book.
- Expect the summary to be written in an overly effusive style.

Flip through the pages.

- Look for how the typeface is arranged.
- Is there a lack of white space or considerable dialogue?
- Are the chapters short or long?

Read the first chapter.

- Determine the story's pacing.
- How are the characters introduced?

Skim other sections of the book at random.

- How does the story seem to flow?
- Are you able to get a sense of plot development?
- Do you regularly encounter new characters?

Read the last chapter.

- Does the story reach a conclusive ending?
- Do you suspect a sequel is in the works?

---

information and recreational needs. Consequently, a three-tiered model as described in table 6.2 has found its way into many libraries.

CLASSES AND INFORMAL INSTRUCTION

Formal instruction takes place in a structured environment. It typically involves a classroom situation with a limited number of participants or is provided as a one-on-one activity. Classes generally focus on a single topic while one-on-one sessions may cover several topics based on what and how much an individual wishes to learn. The key goal is to create an atmosphere conducive to learning, where interruptions and extraneous noise are avoided or kept to a minimum.

Libraries offer classes on a scheduled basis on a variety of topics, including general computer use, operating systems, word processing, spreadsheets, e-mail, searching the Internet, and more. Intermediate- and advanced-level classes are sometimes offered as a follow-up where demand exists. Most classes follow a carefully prepared script and involve hands-on activities and exercises. They generally last from sixty to ninety minutes. Class materials may be prepared in-house by staff or adapted from other sources, such as a resource library or public library system. Unfortunately, many small libraries may lack the resources—staffing,

	Service orientation	
Square footage allocation	**Purpose**	**Design**
Minimum (35)	• Individual use • "Express" (self-service) checkout • Self-service holds checkout • "Express" Internet station (e.g., 10-minute time limit) • Search online catalog, check e-mail	• Stand-up (i.e., no chair or stool provided) • Small counter space • Easily accessible from a service desk
Moderate (45)	• Individual use (for maximum time allowed per library policy) • Internet searching, word processing, filling out online forms/applications, games	• Seating provided • Counter space for papers, books, etc. • Easily accessible from a service desk
Optimum (50)	• Small-group or individual uses • Extended use • Specified use (e.g., job center, employment-related activities) • Selected examples: study groups, tutors, one-on-one instruction	• Appropriately sized furnishings • Enclosed, soundproof space works best in this situation • Located away from library's high-traffic areas

TABLE 6.2 : Public access computer stations, square footage, and service orientation

meeting room space, sufficient equipment, high-speed Internet access—to offer classes even on an occasional basis.

Some libraries have learned that offering one-on-one computer instruction sessions, or tutorials, is a better use of staff resources, particularly if there has been a problem with people preregistering for classes and then not showing up. One-on-one instruction still requires advance registration, as libraries will reserve specific blocks of time for this service during the week or month. Offering this service on a drop-in basis is likely to be too disruptive. Sessions generally run for thirty minutes and cover topics similar to what is presented in a classroom setting. The main advantage to one-on-one instruction is flexibility, in both the content and pace of the tutorial.

Informal instruction, on the other hand, is a part of the give-and-take that occurs during a reference interview. While assisting a patron in finding the information he needs, the librarian does more than point him in the right direction. She moves away from the desk and goes with the patron to a computer station or a section of shelving and briefly describes the search strategy she is using. For someone unfamiliar with a particular aspect of library service, a brief tutorial is in order.

One-on-one computer assistance brochure

SUMMER 2009
Need a little One-on-One computer assistance?

Trying to open an email account?

Need to add bullet points to your resume?

Want a quick lesson in finding old newspaper articles online?

The Middleton Public Library Reference Staff is here to help!

You can make an appointment to ensure a 30 minute tutorial with our staff on the following dates during the hours notes (please see other side for the topics offered):

Thursday, 6/25	3pm–5pm
Monday, 6/29	5pm–7pm
Tuesday, 7/7	4pm–6pm
Thursday, 7/16	3pm–5pm
Monday, 7/20	5pm–7pm

To make an appointment call 827-7403; stop by the library's Reference Desk; or email mid@scls.lib.wi.us.

* SEE OTHER SIDE FOR TOPICS *

SUMMER 2009
30-minute-or-less computer topics that you can sign up for on Middleton Public Library's "one-on-one Fridays."

(see other side for details!)

• How to use a mouse
• Signing up for an email account
• Opening and attaching email files
• Scanning photographs (& basic editing)
• Placing holds in LINKcat
• Accessing full-text magazine & newspaper articles online
• Sprucing up your resume with bullet points, boxes, and shading

For appointments call 827-7403
MIDDLETON PUBLIC LIBRARY
7425 Hubbard Avenue
Middleton WI 53562

A member of the South Central Library System

Here's an illustrative example.

Imagine that a middle-aged man approaches a service desk and begins his reference query as follows. "I need to find a magazine article and don't have the slightest idea how to begin. I know you folks don't have *Reader's Guide* anymore."

Although it's rarely advisable to make assumptions in reference work, it's likely in this case that the patron hasn't used a library for his stated purpose since high school. He is, however, aware that there are resources available to help him out.

The easiest, and not recommended, approach to this request for assistance is to stand in place and offer directions with a pointed finger. "You can search for magazine articles in full text now by using one of our computers. There's an open one over there. Just click on the link that says 'databases.'"

Full text . . . link . . . databases . . .

By this time, the patron may have forgotten why he visited the library in the first place. The response he received did not inform or provide instruction.

Here's the recommended response. "Yes, it's been awhile since we've kept *Reader's Guide* on the shelves. Fortunately, there have been many improvements since those days. Let me get you started on this computer over here."

At this point, the librarian goes with the patron and conducts a thorough reference interview in order to elicit the exact nature of the patron's information need. In this case, she hopes to pinpoint the article's title or subject matter, as well as the name and date of the magazine in which it appeared, if possible. She provides a brief demonstration of how to search the database, select the article from the search results, and, if necessary, print a copy. Before returning to the service desk, she encourages the patron to request follow-up assistance and is sure to ask the question, "Did you find what you needed?" before he leaves the library.

This little scenario describes the important practice of informal instruction in the library. With so much information found online, it's an increasingly key element of a successful reference interview.

OUTREACH SERVICES

Outreach services expand the library's boundaries. By extending its reach beyond its physical walls, a library provides services to those who otherwise might not use them. Such service extension connects with those who are unable to leave their residence due to physical infirmity or who lack the transportation to travel to the library on their own. In addition, outreach allows the library to work with other community agencies to support and enhance programs of mutual interest, such as early literacy or English as a new language.

A traditional example of outreach services is the regularly scheduled delivery of materials to a community's nursing homes, continuing care centers, and senior center. Based on input provided by facility coordinators, who generally serve as the library's contacts for this service, library staff prepare boxes of materials that are delivered to the participating locations on a monthly basis. General subject area and specific title requests are also solicited from residents and clients. Library volunteers often provide invaluable assistance in the implementation of this program.

The Five Elements of the Reference Interview

These five basic elements provide useful behavioral guidelines for most patron interactions in the library, not just for standard reference queries.

Approachability

1. Smiles.
2. Makes eye contact.
3. Gives a friendly greeting.

Comfort

1. Maintains eye contact.
2. Body looks attentive and relaxed.
3. Speaks in interested, helpful tone.
4. Speaks slowly and clearly.

Interest

1. Gives patron full attention.
2. Listens attentively.
3. Makes appropriate comments.
4. Goes with patron.

Negotiation

1. Asks open questions/probes for information ("What specific information are you looking for?").
2. Paraphrases/clarifies.
3. Uses encouragers.
4. Informs.
5. Summarizes.
6. Uses the resources at hand.
7. Goes beyond immediate resources.
8. Cites the source.

Follow-up

1. "Does this answer your question?"
2. "Did you find what you were looking for?"
3. Closes the interview tactfully.

Source: Elaine Z. Jennerich and Edward J. Jennerich, *The Reference Interview as a Creative Art*, 2nd edition (Libraries Unlimited, 1997).

Books-by-mail, or homebound delivery, is a similar type of service, though it provides an opportunity for more individualized service. It is typically offered to area residents who are unable to travel to the library due to temporary or permanent disability, age, or illness. An application allows the participant to specify formats (e.g., large print, audiobooks on CD), the quantity to be sent at any one time, reading preferences, and language preference. Some libraries require the signature of a physician, nurse, or social worker on the application in order to qualify users for this service.

Another common example of outreach involves service to local jails. In setting up this type of service, the library negotiates with a county or local correctional facility to determine where the jail library will be located, when it will be open for service, and who will provide the funding for materials, shelving, and furnishings. In most cases, library staff take responsibility for the jail library's ongoing operation. Additionally, its collection is often supplemented by donations from a Friends group, used-book stores, and individuals.

The presence of a library in a correctional facility provides inmates an opportunity to put their incarceration time to more productive use, thus lessening their feelings of idleness and boredom. Through special requests, it also gives inmates access to educational materials for self-improvement and legal materials related to their criminal cases.

COMMUNITY USE OF LIBRARY SPACES

MEETING ROOMS

In many communities, the public library may offer the only free or low-cost meeting room space for use by the public. For this reason, requests for information are likely a source of potential conflicts if not handled in a prescribed and consistent manner. To ensure fair and equitable use, a clear and concise policy that outlines board-approved guidelines for use must be established and well publicized.

According to Article VI of the Library Bill of Rights, meeting rooms should be available to the public "on an equitable basis, regardless of the beliefs or affiliations of individuals or groups requesting their use." In other words, the language in a library's meeting room policy should be inclusive rather than exclusive. That being said, a policy may include qualifying statements regarding the time, location, and manner of use. The library, for example, may offer use of its meeting room only during its regularly scheduled hours of operation. Furthermore, in order to provide this service to the widest possible audience, the library may impose a limit on the number of reservations allowed during a particular time period. ("Use of the room by any organization is limited to one meeting per month.") In addition, it may include a statement indicating that any use must not interfere with the regular operation of the library. Requests, however, should not be denied because of the subject matter of a group's program or meeting. For this reason, the policy should include the following disclaimer: "The library does not advocate or endorse the viewpoints of meetings or meeting room users."

An effective meeting room policy also addresses specific exemptions and prohibitions. The most common type of exemption occurs when a library gives priority to and imposes no limits on the scheduling of its own programs. This courtesy is usually extended to functions sponsored by the municipality in which the library is located. A library typically prohibits

Fewer Bookmobiles on the Road

Dane County Bookmobile at the Paoli, Wisconsin, town square

According to *Famous First Facts*, the first "bookwagon traveling library," a precursor to the book-mobile, was introduced in 1905 by the Washington County Free Library in Hagerstown, Maryland. A former grocery wagon was refitted with bookshelves and followed a schedule of stops throughout the county three times a week. The driver was the library's janitor.

Bookmobiles have historically served rural areas but inevitably made inroads into some urban centers, particularly in neighborhoods lacking a branch location. The New Orleans Public Library, for example, has used bookmobile service as a way to reach areas of the community in the aftermath of Hurricane Katrina.

The number of bookmobiles on the road reached its peak in the 1960s. A steady decline began in the early 1970s as a result of a sharp increase in gasoline prices. This development forced some libraries to rethink their methods of service delivery.

The following table shows the total number of bookmobiles in operation since 1935.

Year	Number
1935	25
1950	550
1954	900
1963	1,400
1965	2,000
1992	1,000
2007	864

As of 2007, Kentucky led all other states with 98 bookmobiles in operation.

TALES FROM THE FIELD: Outreach Services 101—What is the best approach to outreach services into the community for small libraries?

Library personnel are the greatest resource in providing outreach services to those with special needs or underserved populations in your community. A staff member open to serving those in need of special services may identify opportunities for the library as well as engage in problem-solving to meet the needs of patrons.

Raise awareness about serving patrons with special needs among library staff members. Whether yours is a one-person library or you have ten staff members or more, invite an advocate to your library to talk about adults and children with special needs and ask this person to demonstrate adaptive equipment.

The more your staff know about special needs issues, the easier it will be for them to assist individuals who seek accommodations. Where to find someone to talk to your staff? From your list of "go to" resources.

A list of resources not only provides potential trainers for your staff but also alleviates the stress of trying to determine who to contact when someone phones or walks through the door with an accommodation request. When putting together the list, begin in your own community. Seek out individuals with experience in the area of special needs. Identify the special needs consultant in your library system and state library. The American Library Association Office for Literacy and Outreach Services offers many resources on its website. Identify organizations serving individuals with special needs in the community: they may be regional or statewide organizations. In addition, remember the Library for the Blind and Physically Handicapped office serving your community. In some states, the name includes the words *braille and talking book library*. Staff members of the Library for the Blind are often looking for opportunities to talk to public library staff members in order to promote use of the service.

Ever hear of a grocery store shopping cart as a bookmobile? The Butler (Wisconsin) Public Library used a shopping cart donated by a local grocery store to deliver to residents of senior apartments who couldn't get to the library. To check out the books, a handheld Palm with a scanner was provided by the library system. The library system purchased the device with LSTA funds. A new delivery system is being planned because new volunteers have agreed to deliver books, and they prefer not to use the shopping cart.

Pauline Haass Public Library in Sussex, Wisconsin, offers its meeting room to a group of local job seekers. A library staff member gets the discussion going by asking how the job hunting has gone since they last met, and each participant talks about his or her experiences. Not only do participants learn from one another, they receive suggestions from the library staff member as to resources the library has to assist them.

The Alice Baker Memorial Library in Eagle, Wisconsin, partners with the local school district outreach tutor who works with at-risk students unable to attend school. The tutor meets students at the library, and library staff assist students when they are learning research techniques.

Source: Nancy Fletcher, PR and Special Needs Librarian, Waukesha County (Wisconsin) Library System.

---

meeting room users from charging fees or soliciting donations. In other words, events are free and open to the public.

For guidelines not directly addressed in the policy itself, library staff may wish to create a promotional brochure that includes answers to the questions most likely to be asked about meeting room availability, capacity, furnishings, and other amenities.

Booking a room. Whom do I contact? Do I have to register in person or can I do so online? Do I need to have a library card? How far in advance may I reserve a room? Do I need a key?

Charges for use. Does it cost anything to use a room? Do I need to make a deposit? What happens if we damage something? (Also an opportunity to address acceptable uses.)

Room size and access. How many people will the room accommodate? Is the room handicapped-accessible? Is there a separate entrance?

Room setup. What types of furnishings are available? Can the room be arranged theater-style? Is there someone at the library to help us set up tables and chairs?

Equipment. Does the room have a podium and microphone? Is wireless Internet access available? Do we have to bring our own computer?

Food and drink. Does the meeting room have kitchen facilities? Is it okay to have a meal brought in?

Having copies of the library's meeting room policy or a promotional brochure available for easy access at a service desk is an effective way to help staff feel confident when answering questions and avoid giving out misinformation.

EXHIBIT SPACE

Use of a library's exhibit space should be handled in a manner similar to that for meeting room use. An effective library policy conforms to the Library Bill of Rights and addresses the issue of fair and equitable access and the aim to represent a diversity of views.

Exhibit space includes but is not limited to built-in and stand-alone display cases, freestanding displays, picture rails, and bulletin boards. This last method of display, however, is typically used to post announcements of community events and activities according to established guidelines, such as the size of the notice and the length of time it may be displayed. In most small public libraries, the amount of exhibit space available for public use will be limited. Because of the time involved in setting up and taking down displays, libraries generally book their exhibit space for one-month intervals. Providing this service works best when responsibilities are assigned to an individual staff person.

For displays of artwork or other items of value, the exhibitor should be required to sign a release or waiver form that exempts the library from responsibility for loss, damage, or destruction while the items are in the possession of the library.

PROMOTING SERVICES AND PROGRAMS

Through the use of old media (newspapers, radio, television, advertising flyers) and new media (websites, blogs, e-mail, social networks, YouTube), library staff have numerous means at their disposal to develop an effective public relations and marketing program. Promoting the library's services and programs no longer depends on a drawn-out process of request forms, a series of editing and proofreading deadlines, and wait time for delivery. With desktop

---

Sample Meeting Room Policy

Purpose

The meeting rooms of the _____ Public Library are available for use by community groups and organizations for informational, educational, or recreational meetings and programs in keeping with the mission of the library.

Guidelines

1. Meeting room facilities will be made available during the library's regular hours of operation on an equitable basis, regardless of the beliefs or affiliations of individuals or groups requesting their use.

2. Meetings are scheduled on a first-come, first-served basis.

3. Rooms may be used for:

   meetings that are open to the public

   public lectures, panel discussions, film and slide presentations, group discussions, workshops, and other similar functions

   organizations or individuals engaged in educational, cultural, intellectual, governmental, or charitable activities

4. Rooms may not be used for:

   any purpose that may interfere with the regular operation of the library

   programs involving the sale, advertising, solicitation, or promotion of commercial products or services

   personal, company, or family parties

5. No single group may have more than three (3) meetings reserved in advance. Exceptions are library- or library system-sponsored programs and those offered by [the municipality or county], which receive priority in scheduling.

6. No admission fee, registration fee, or donations may be sought from meeting attendees, except by local nonprofit educational, social service, or cultural organizations with the specific permission of the library director. This guideline is waived for library fund-raising activities and for fees associated with functions sponsored by [the municipality/county].

7. No charge will be made by the library for the use of the meeting rooms.

8. Users agree to abide by all regulations of the library relating to the use of the facilities and accept responsibility for all damages caused to the building and/or equipment beyond normal wear.

9. Use of the library meeting rooms does not imply endorsement by the library staff or trustees of the viewpoints presented.

---

publishing software and social media, getting the word out becomes a daily activity of the library's operations.

The following paragraphs provide brief definitions of public relations and marketing and examples of how these promotional tools can be used to a library's advantage.

PUBLIC RELATIONS

In very basic terms, public relations tells your audience who you are and what you do. More specifically, it is a planned, public information program that consists of a variety of activities

---

Sample Exhibits Policy

Purpose

In order to provide as many attractive, educational, and cultural exhibits as possible for the benefit of the community, the library provides exhibition space for community groups, organizations, schools, and individuals.

Description of Exhibit Space

1. A locked display case is available for monthly bookings only.

2. A picture rail is available for scheduled exhibits. Freestanding exhibits may be displayed in areas of the library that do not interfere with library services or traffic patterns. These requests will be reviewed on a case-by-case basis by the library director.

Guidelines

1. Exhibits must contribute to the general appearance of the library facility.

2. Exhibits must not interfere with the general operation of regular library activities.

3. Information presented in exhibits shall be governed by the spirit of the Library Bill of Rights and freedom of information concepts.

4. The library does not advocate or endorse the viewpoints of exhibits or exhibitors.

5. It is the responsibility of the exhibitor to set up and remove the exhibits at scheduled times.

6. The library director shall accept requests and grant permission to set up exhibits.

7. The library director has the final decision on the content and arrangement of all exhibits.

8. All publicity material relating to exhibits shall be submitted to the library director for approval.

9. Items on exhibit that are available for purchase may not have prices noted. Exhibitors may display an explanation of the exhibit and provide contact information.

---

designed to establish and maintain contact with those whom the library serves. Put another way, it's a means by which library staff explain and highlight the library's mission statement (e.g., "to make a positive difference in the quality of life in our community") with concrete examples. Public relations, particularly as it is used by libraries, is primarily a one-way communication process, a means to get the word out, tell the library's story, and raise the visibility of its services and programs. For the most part, little consideration is given to what the target audience needs or wants to hear.

Examples of "old media" public relations:

Newspapers have long provided an outlet for announcements of programs, descriptions of new or enhanced services, and reviews of new books and audiovisual materials. Particularly in small communities where the daily or weekly paper emphasizes local news, a regularly appearing column of timely topics written by the director or other staff members remains an effective way to get the word out.

Radio provides an opportunity to broadcast public service announcements on a regular basis, although they are not likely to be aired during prime listening periods.

Sample Exhibit Release Form

I, the undersigned, hereby lend the following works of art or other material to the _____ Public Library for exhibit purposes only. In consideration of the privilege of exhibiting them in the Library, I hereby release said Library from responsibility for loss, damage, or destruction while they are in the possession of the Library.

Exhibition to be held in the _____

During _____

Description of materials loaned _____

Signature _____ Date _____

Address _____ Telephone _____

Staff should volunteer to be guests on local talk shows, particularly if the host uses a standard question-and-answer interview format. A scheduled block of airtime for reviews of new materials and announcements of upcoming programs is an effective way to promote the library's services.

Television is a good choice for special events coverage, such as a summer reading program kick-off or an anniversary celebration.

Advertising flyers are informational guides of all types, printed in bulk. They include brochures, bookmarks, and one-sheet or half-sheet promos that cover the gamut of library services. These may be done in-house with desktop publishing software or outsourced to a library system or commercial printer.

Examples of "new media" public relations:

Websites. The cardinal rule of library home page design is to highlight location, hours of operation, and contact information. In addition, the home page should include prominently placed links to information about services and programs and a monthly calendar of events, perhaps with the option of online registration for programs.

Blogs. Libraries are increasingly using blogs as the template for their websites, providing their patrons, and anyone else who cares to check in, with a colorful daily diary of news and events.

E-mail provides an opportunity to create mailing lists tailored to individual interests and needs: new materials, programs, storytime registration, Friends of the Library book sales, board meetings, weather-related or other emergency closings. An increasing number of municipalities are using automated communications systems to get the word out about all activities related to local government, including the library.

Social networks. Twitter, Facebook, and Flickr accounts are easy to set up and maintain. They provide an effective way to reduce dependency on traditional in-house methods of promoting library services and programs—or to share information about the community.

YouTube. The options here are limitless. A few examples: a virtual tour of the library facility, full video or snippets from a storytime session or other library program (with presenters' permission, of course), library tutorials (how to place a hold in the online catalog, how to download an audiobook).

MARKETING

Marketing differs from public relations in that it is a two-way communication process. The library attempts to create a dialogue with its audience. In both formal and informal settings, information is gathered by asking people what services, programs, and other amenities they value and how those can effectively be delivered. The library then uses this information both to enhance current offerings and to meet changing needs.

The methods used for this type of information gathering range from the simple and cheap to the laborious and expensive. The following examples are listed in order of the easiest to the most difficult to carry out.

Comment forms offer a way for library users to provide written feedback about the library's operations. Forms are made available in both paper and electronic format. One advantage of this admittedly casual method of marketing is that it allows for anonymity, although space should be provided on the form for the inclusion of the person's name and contact information. In this way, a staff member may follow up on a particular concern or request. The use of comment forms is likely to touch on a broad range of issues, including collection development, display of materials, staff–patron interactions, computer use, policy concerns, inappropriate behaviors, and the arrangement of the library's floor plan. Over time, comment forms are likely to pinpoint where the delivery of library services needs to be reviewed: lack of sufficient staffing at a service desk, or the need for more or faster access to the Internet, or the desire for a separate display of new audiovisual materials. After any modifications or enhancements have been made as a result of this collective input, the library may want to highlight its responses with a "You Asked, We Listened" promotion.

Another casual method of marketing involves the use of *steno notebooks,* one of which is kept at each service desk in the library. Staff members are encouraged to summarize comments that are shared while checking out materials or otherwise providing assistance. Some library patrons are comfortable offering their suggestions and concerns face-to-face, and often the comments will mirror those that are collected through written forms. More commonly, though, what's on patrons' minds is how much they appreciate the library and the services and programs it provides, and they offer their praises in the most glowing terms. The most eloquent of these statements should, in turn, be shared with board members and elected officials during budget deliberations, planning sessions, and other discussions about the importance of library services in the community. A staff *wiki* may also be used for the purpose of collecting library patron comments.

Admittedly, written and "across-the-desk" comments are unscientific approaches to gathering information for marketing purposes. Nevertheless, they provide a relatively easy and effective way to strengthen customer relations and improve library services.

FOCUS GROUPS

Merriam-Webster's Collegiate Dictionary defines the term *focus group* as "a small group of people whose response to something (as a new product or a politician's image) is studied to determine the response that can be expected from a larger population." Though not a scientifically rigorous method of gathering information, focus groups allow libraries to gain feedback about library services and to discern perceptions about the library itself from both user and nonuser groups. Unlike formal telephone surveys of randomly selected participants, the process is a relatively inexpensive one to implement but will require a significant investment of time on the part of the library staff and board. In addition to providing feedback about library services and programs, focus groups offer an effective way to determine how successful the library has been in getting the word out.

Setting up a successful series of focus group discussions requires five steps.

1. *Hire a consultant.* To ensure that participants feel comfortable to speak freely, a consultant should be hired to conduct each focus group session. The facilitator of these discussions needs to be perceived as library-neutral. In some cases, a consultant may wish to have a recorder available to transcribe each of the sessions, which, unless otherwise negotiated, is a responsibility that falls to the library.

2. *Develop a list of questions.* The consultant assists the library with this part of the project, providing suggestions as to the wording, number (no more than seven),

---

Sample Comment Form

Your thoughts about the library are very important to us. Please take a moment to share your ideas and concerns about any aspect of the library's services, programs, and facility. If you would like a personal reply, please include your name and the preferred method of contact. Please deposit this form in the Comment Box located at the circulation desk.

Please complete the following if you would like a personal reply:

Name _____

Address _____

Phone number _____ E-mail _____

THANK YOU FOR YOUR INPUT!

Sample Focus Group Discussion Questions

1. "Round-robin" introductions of participants.

2. Tell us what you did during your last visit (in person or electronically) to the library.

3. What do you think the library does really well?

4. What suggestions do you have for improving the library?

5. I've heard there's some discussion about an expansion for the library. Do you think that's a good idea? Why or why not?

6. The library plans to devote more of its materials budget to digital media—downloadable books, movies, and music. Is this something you would favor? Why or why not?

7. Anything else? [Final say]

---

and flow of the questions. It is incumbent upon the library board and staff, however, to determine what they wish to learn from these sessions.

3. *Select who will participate, schedule the sessions, and send out invitations.* Depending on the number of focus group sessions scheduled (four to six is considered optimum), the library is responsible for developing a list of potential participants, determining when the sessions take place (preferably over a period of less than two weeks), drafting a letter of invitation, keeping track of responses once the invitations have been mailed, and sending out last-minute reminder notices.

4. *Conduct the sessions.* Prior to the arrival of the consultant, and well before the arrival of the participants, library staff need to set up the room, provide clear signage to its location, and provide light refreshments—determine that everything is in place to proceed smoothly, in other words.

5. *Publicize and use the findings.* When the consultant has provided the library with a final report, the director prepares a summary of its findings, which is given wide distribution via both old and new media. In addition, the director, in conjunction with the library board president, makes a formal presentation to municipal or county officials, or to both.

Using a variety of promotional methods to get the word out about services and programs helps to increase the library's visibility in the community. In addition, a well-developed program of public relations and marketing serves to position the library as an essential service, a particularly important consideration in an increasingly competitive environment for financial support.

NOTES

1. Charles R. McClure et al., *Planning and Role Setting for Public Libraries: A Manual of Options and Procedures* (Chicago: American Library Association, 1987), 28.

2. Annabel K. Stephens, *Assessing the Public Library Planning Process* (New York: Ablex Publishing, 1995), 75.

3. Ethel E. Himmel, *Planning for Results. [Vol. 1], The Guidebook: A Public Library Transformation Process* (Chicago: American Library Association, 1998).

4. Darlene E. Weingand, *Administration of the Small Public Library* (Chicago: American Library Association, 2001), 54.

5. Philip Kotler, *Marketing for Nonprofit Organizations,* 2nd edition (Englewood Cliffs, NJ: Prentice-Hall, 1982), 289.

6. Weingand, *Administration of the Small Public Library.*

7. Barbara Will Razzano, "Creating the Library Habit," *Library Journal,* February 15, 1985.

8. Ibid.

9. Ibid., 114.

10. Institute of Museum and Library Services, *Public Libraries in the United States: Fiscal Year 2008,* http://harvester.census.gov/imls/pubs/pls/pub_detail.asp?id=130.

11. Institute of Museum and Library Services, *Public Libraries in the United States: Fiscal Year 2000,* http://harvester.census.gov/imls/pubs/pls/pub_detail.asp?id=55.

12. Institute of Museum and Library Services, *Public Libraries in the United States: Fiscal Year 2008,* http://harvester.census.gov/imls/pubs/pls/pub_detail.asp?id=130.

13. Samuel Swett Green, "Personal Relations between Librarians and Readers," *American Library Journal* 1 (October 1876): 74–81.

14. Bill Crowley, "Rediscovering the History of Readers Advisory Service," *Public Libraries* 44, no. 1 (2005): 37–41.

15. Anders Dahlgren, *Public Library Space Needs: A Planning Outline* (Madison: Wisconsin Department of Public Instruction, 2009).

CHAPTER SEVEN

THE LIBRARY AS PLACE

DEVELOPING A COMMUNITY-CENTERED PHILOSOPHY —

Your public library—recreational activity or essential service? Who makes the call?

Unfortunately, it doesn't appear to be the library director or members of the library board who are driving this decision, for the most part.

Historically, public libraries have frequently been lumped together with such seasonal services as parks, swimming pools, and golf courses as an element of municipal and county organization. Hence, libraries are generally recognized as a recreational activity, most particularly during a period when equalized property tax values decrease and the collection of tax revenue shrinks. When budget cuts are up for discussion, library services are often one of the first areas to receive attention. Efforts need to be made to reposition the public library in the minds of local and county officials. The focus, however, should not be on how the library is categorized in a budget document but, rather, how it is positioned in the community itself.

Let's say that someone asks you to describe, in ten words or less, why the public library continues to play an important role in the lives of its community members. Or perhaps more likely, you are confronted with the oft-heard observation, "Why do we need libraries when we have the Internet?" How would you answer either of these questions? In other words, what is your vision of the library? Your response must succinctly clarify why library services are essential to a community's cultural and economic well-being.

Best answer? "Libraries are at the heart of our communities." And there are so many positive examples that you can use to elaborate on this statement.

Support for this concept of the public library as a vital and essential service was recently offered by what some might consider an unexpected source. The cover story of the summer

2009 issue of the *Planning Commissioners Journal* promotes the idea of "Libraries at the Heart of Our Communities." Published quarterly, the *Planning Commissioners Journal* aims to reach an audience of citizen planners, as well as members of local planning commissions and zoning boards—individuals, in other words, who are likely to have a say about library building and remodeling projects.

Author and editor Wayne Senville opens his article with a series of questions (and they are very easy questions to answer).

Is there a place in your community

- where residents of all ages and incomes visit and enjoy spending their time?
- where people go to hear interesting speakers discuss new ideas, books, travel, and a broad range of topics?
- where comprehensive databases are available free of charge?
- where you can get help when applying for a job?
- where you can stop by and take home a book, CD, or DVD at virtually no cost?

That's also a place

- that's "owned" by everyone in the community?
- and can be counted on, day after day, to draw people downtown or to Main Street?

In a growing number of cities and towns, there's one answer to all these questions: the public library.[1]

Senville goes on to describe public libraries as the anchors of U.S. cities and towns, places that help to revitalize downtown and neighborhoods.

The idea of using libraries as a catalyst for economic development has served the city of Chicago extremely well. A partnership formed by Mayor Richard M. Daley and Library Commissioner Mary Dempsey has transformed the library's branch systems and rejuvenated neighborhoods. An *American Libraries* article summarized the results as follows:

> Today the nondescript storefronts and dilapidated buildings that once characterized the Chicago Public Library system are largely gone. Almost 70% of its 76 branches are new or extensively renovated, full-service libraries. In neighborhood after neighborhood, Chicago's new libraries have demonstrated their power to transform. Not only does library use soar, the neighborhoods themselves are revitalized. Aldermen now vie to have new or renovated libraries in their neighborhoods—and community residents sing their praises.[2]

In other words, the branches of the Chicago Public Library have become the hearts of their neighborhood communities.

This power of libraries to transform their communities is not limited to large urban centers. The city of DeForest, Wisconsin (population 9,058), has a similar story to tell. In 2002, the DeForest Public Library opened a 35,000-square-foot downtown location, which quickly became one of the most popular destinations in town, drawing more than 200,000 visitors annually.

Libraries as "Anchor Store"

The Wisconsin Council on Libraries and Network Development, an advisory committee to the State Superintendent of Public Instruction and the administrator of the Division for Libraries, Technology, and Community Learning, has endorsed the "anchor store" concept in its "Beginnings Report on the Future of Wisconsin Libraries, 2008–2018."

Strategic Direction 3. Libraries as "anchor store"
Urban and rural communities across the country have strategically placed public libraries to stimulate economic development, improve the safety of neighborhoods, and improve literacy for [their] citizens. In schools and universities, libraries serve as an anchor for intellectual development. In the private sector, such as health care, library/information centers educate and serve the information needs of their clients.

Wisconsin will expand and promote the anchor store concept for strategic use throughout the state. By 2010 Wisconsin libraries will be recognized as community development engines, providing knowledge resources and community gathering spaces, attracting business to the area.

[The] Department of Public Instruction should expand the impact of [the] Student Learning through Wisconsin School Libraries study by demonstrating the fiscal impact of increased educational attainment fostered by quality school librarians.

Objective 1. Find and publicize "anchor store" success stories from all types of libraries, and connect to the WLA "Campaign for Wisconsin Libraries."

Objective 2. Educate library trustees, school boards, and other governing bodies about the "anchor store" concept.

Objective 3. Look for opportunities for government investment (federal, state, regional, local) in the "anchor store" concept to develop Wisconsin economy and communities.

Objective 4. Publicize results of Economic Impact of Wisconsin Public Libraries: fourfold return on investment.

An article in the *DeForest Times-Tribune* chronicles the change.

> Like the appearance of the library, from its cramped space in the strip mall north of the post office to its unique Scandinavian-style downtown centerpiece, the entire downtown district has put on a new face over the past decade. It's almost hard to envision some of the dilapidated buildings and grain towers that once occupied the approximately four-block area which has been redeveloped into the bustling residential and commercial center of downtown DeForest.[3]

A new library leads to further downtown redevelopment. As a result, the DeForest Public Library has become the heart of its community, pumping life into a once forlorn and dilapidated area.

In an essay by *Washington Post* syndicated columnist Neal Peirce, libraries are described as the "enablers of generations of Americans' dreams," reaching out to new immigrants to provide English instruction, study rooms for tutoring, and other specialized services. Offering public access computers and assistance with job searches are just two elements of what Peirce refers to as a "great historic transformation." As Audra Caplan, director of the Harford County (Maryland) Public Library and 2010 president of the Public Library Association, tells him:

> We've turned ourselves into community centers. We have meeting rooms that get booked by community agencies, chess clubs, any not-for-profit. We bring in authors, we sponsor civic engagement-type programs. And we're attracting a larger share of the population—even teens, or parents with toddlers.[4]

All libraries—urban, suburban, and rural—are well served when library staff, board members, and other advocates continuously promote the vital importance of libraries and describe how they enhance community life. Any plan for the library's future must include an emphasis that libraries are indeed at the heart of our communities.

LIBRARY ADVOCACY

An effective program of advocacy begins inside the building, as the library's most outspoken supporters are likely to be regular and enthusiastic consumers of its services. Without a welcoming atmosphere and a helpful staff, the library has no solid foundation on which to build. The director needs to ensure that the distribution of goodwill begins at a library's service desk. In order to accomplish this goal, staff need to use positive customer service strategies.

Staff can help to create a strong foundation by following these basic guidelines:

- Be approachable. (Be aware of your surroundings while working at a service desk.)
- Welcome people to the library. (Smile, make eye contact, offer a greeting.)
- Treat everyone with courtesy and respect.
- Ask people, "Are you finding (did you find) what you were looking for?"

Word-of-Mouth Marketing (WOMM)

In very general terms, word-of-mouth marketing is defined as an unpaid form of promotion in which satisfied customers tell other people how much they like a business, product, or service.

Why should libraries be interested in this approach to marketing their services and programs? Peggy Barber and Linda Wallace provide three compelling reasons in "The Power of Word-of-Mouth Marketing," originally posted on the *American Libraries* website on October 26, 2009.

> *We think WOMM makes sense for libraries for three very good reasons. One, because we can afford it. For the first time, the playing field is level. We can compete. We can win public awareness and support. Two, libraries have a potential sales force of millions, including our entire staffs, Friends, trustees, and satisfied customers who for the most part we have not tapped. And three, because it absolutely is the most powerful form of communication.*

The library's advocacy message will reach more receptive ears if the library has already created positive and wide-ranging "word-of-mouth marketing" for its services and programs. The overall guiding principle for library staff is summed up as follows: Service to patrons is not an interruption of work but, rather, the purpose for it. In other words, the goal is to ensure that people leave your facility in a very favorable frame of mind once they have checked out a book or used a computer or attended a program or visited the library for whatever other reasons. In fact, not only are they pleased with the outcome, but they can't wait to tell a friend or colleague about the experience.

The American Library Association (ALA) promotes the idea that library advocacy is a front-line activity, one that involves every level of staff.[5] The following annotated checklists, adapted from ALA's "Library Advocacy Now" web pages, provide suggestions as to how board members and Friends of the Library can build upon the library's advocacy foundation.

How library board members contribute:

> Use political savvy and community connections on behalf of the library. (Note to director: Have the names of prospective board members on file. Recruit community members whose skills match the library's need—for example, strategic planning, public relations, organizational behavior, policy development, regional cooperation.)

> Make a point of getting to know key officials. (Look for opportunities outside the library. For example, a board member and a council member might belong to the same service club or church or have children who are in the same grade in school or play on the same athletic team.)

> Stay in touch even when not asking for something. (Attending council meetings on a round-robin basis provides library board members with the opportunity for informal contacts before and after each meeting.)

> Work closely with the library director in developing advocacy messages and strategies. (And be willing to follow through on them.)

> And in conjunction with the previous point, develop official responses to questions that might arise about the library's operations, particularly in regard to any sensitive library issue, such as age-appropriate library materials. (Nothing derails the goodwill an organization has developed faster than spokespersons sending out confused and conflicting messages.)

> Join your state library association's trustee organization. (Through contacts with colleagues throughout the state, trustees stay informed about the bigger picture of libraries. And learn from each other's successes—and mistakes.)

How Friends of the Library contribute:

> Work in cooperation with the library staff and board. (The library director should either serve as a liaison to the Friends of the Library or delegate this responsibility to an appropriate staff member. In addition, the practice of inviting Friends board members to a library board meeting on an annual basis, with specific

discussion items noted on the agenda, is a good one to establish. Whatever the connections, there needs to be clear agreement on how any funds the Friends raise are expended. The staff, board, and Friends need to always work as a team.)

Build public awareness and support for the library. (Membership and participation in the activities of the local chamber of commerce are excellent ways to enhance the library's presence in the community.)

Involve community members in Friends' activities. Most Friends groups hold an annual meeting, sponsor library programs, and publish a newsletter. Invite local officials and community leaders to speak to the membership and help to underwrite the cost of programs. And if they're not members, ask them to join. Always be on the lookout for recruits. Use the newsletter to give recognition to those who donate their time and services to the library. All these activities enhance a library's word-of-mouth marketing.

In addition to board and Friends members, library supporters of all stripes can set the stage for advocacy by engaging in a variety of grassroots activities with family members, friends, neighbors, and colleagues. If someone expresses what sounds like a need for help ("I can't get my son to read" or "My daughter isn't sure where to apply for college"), describe the resources available at the library. Provide a contact name and phone number, if you have it. Share personal stories about how libraries benefit people's lives, especially when speaking to community leaders. Speak up for strong financial support of libraries and encourage others to do the same.

In chapter 6 we discussed getting the word out about your library's services and programs. It is easy to fall into a routine of only announcing upcoming programs or publishing lists of new acquisitions. It's also important to build public awareness year-round. ALA's *Communications Handbook for Libraries* offers guidelines for developing a simple but thorough communication plan and reminds us that media attention/publicity can:

- increase public awareness of your programs, personnel, and services
- increase involvement of public and private partners

Association of Library Trustees, Advocates, Friends, and Foundations

ALTAFF is a national network of library supporters who believe in the importance of libraries as the social and intellectual centers of communities and campuses. ALTAFF provides a series of helpful fact sheets on such topics as "Starting a Friends Group," "Revitalizing Your Friends," and "Starting a Friends Foundation," all available at no cost via the American Library Association's website at www.ala.org/ala/mgrps/divs/altaff/index.cfm.

- create, change, build, or enhance the public image of your library
- encourage contributions of money, materials, services, and time
- win support for city, state, federal, foundation, or individual donor funding of your library
- help you to reach new or never before approached audiences, such as non-English speakers
- clarify misunderstandings about what libraries do and how they're financed
- mobilize opinion leaders in your community to become active supporters and advocates of your efforts
- help knit together a vital network of libraries throughout the region, state, and nation and help build public and private support for libraries[6]

Of course it can be challenging to make your publicity interesting month after month. Charlton Laird, speaking to the Iowa Library Conference about "Newspaper Publicity and the Librarian," advised, "Make your publicity news. Tie local people, local events, local history and current events into your stories."[7] That presentation was given in 1927! We have outlets beyond the local newspaper today, but the idea of tying the library's stories to the community's is still pertinent and solidifies the concept that "libraries are at the heart of our communities." Take advantage of promotional materials that have been created for libraries to adapt for local use. Many state library agencies and state library associations support statewide public relations or library promotion campaigns.

The next level of library advocacy takes a more targeted approach. Stay in touch with elected officials and other decision makers. Don't wait until the library is threatened with a budget cut to write, call, or e-mail them and encourage their support of libraries. (Time-tested suggestion: a personal, handwritten note works best. E-mail is less effective.) In addition, library advocates need to take advantage of the various opportunities to speak out in formal settings. Most municipal councils and county boards devote a portion of their meetings to "Comment from Citizens Present." Individuals may address any topic they choose, not just what is listed on the day's agenda. Speakers are generally limited to three to five minutes apiece—plenty of time to deliver an effective library advocacy message.

Three Rules for Winning Support

1. Never assume that others understand what the library does or what it takes to do it. Use every opportunity to educate them.

2. Ask! Research shows that even people who don't use the library appreciate its role and wish to support it.

3. Don't do this alone. Your message is most powerful when others speak up for you.

Source: *The Small but Powerful Guide to Winning Big Support for Your Rural Library*, www.ala.org/ala/aboutala/offices/olos/toolkits/rural_toolkit.pdf.

Elected officials at all levels of government take notice when their constituents speak up on an issue. In some cases, just a handful of contacts might be all it takes to give a specific issue a sense of urgency. For hearings and other forums for public comment regarding budget or other library-related issues, library advocates need to show up, ask questions, voice opinions, and look for support.

A program of library advocacy works best, of course, when supporters send a clear and unified message to elected officials and community leaders. This step of the process is where

---

Tips for Working with Legislators

Your legislator's time is valuable, but he or she appreciates constituent contacts. Here are some ideas for how to most effectively develop an ongoing relationship with your legislator while advocating on behalf of libraries. (These tips work for meeting with any elected official.)

1. *Do Your Homework.* Know the issues and particular interests of your legislator. Keep a background file on your legislators, including special interests and personal profiles. You won't agree on all of the issues all of the time, but a legislator needs to know what constituents are thinking.

2. *Keep in Touch.* Write, call, or visit your legislators and their staff members to introduce yourself. Let them know who you represent and volunteer to keep them informed about your issues, their impact on your community and on the legislator's district.

Add the legislator's name to your mailing list and ask to have your name added to the legislator's mailing list.

Make sure the legislator receives notice of and invitations to special events held at your library. This serves as a reminder of your library's role in the community. Remind your legislator that attending these functions is an excellent way to meet with constituents.

Invite legislators and perhaps their spouses to tour your library. Show them exactly what your library does and how it contributes to community well-being.

3. *Be Consistent and Reliable.* Remember that official policy is set by the Wisconsin Library Association (WLA) Board of Directors. Make clear any differences between your opinions and the position of the WLA. Remember that WLA must be viewed as a credible source of information in order to be successful on behalf of libraries.

It is also not effective to mix discussion of your personal issues with discussion of library issues, or you will dilute your message and confuse the legislator as to your priorities.

4. *Give Credit Where Credit Is Due.* Give public recognition to deserving legislators through awards or at library functions to which your legislator has been invited. Always say "Thank you" for support of your issues. A personal thank-you note is also very effective.

5. *Be a Player.* Attend events, social and other types, at which legislators will be present—not to lobby overtly, but to get acquainted and make them aware of you as an active member of the community. Even if you can afford to give only a small amount of money, attending fund-raisers is an important part of our current political process.

If the legislator has been helpful to your library, get involved in his or her election campaign. People who give their time, and who can recruit others to campaign, are very important to a legislator.

6. *Tell Us about It.* Let WLA know about the concerns and interests your legislator has expressed, along with any commitment of support to library issues.

Source: Developed by the Wisconsin Library Association, with thanks to Citizens for Missouri's Children.

Writing to Legislators

Even in this age of electronic communication, writing a personal letter is still one of the most effective ways to reach an elected official. Taking the time to write about an issue shows you care deeply about it. (Although these instructions are appropriate to use when writing to local and county officials, face-to-face communication is the preferred method of communication with them.)

1. Send your letter in time to affect your legislator's decision.

2. Make sure your letter is easy to read.

3. Use your own words to get your message across. Don't copy a form letter, or even parts of one. If you make the letter entirely your own, your thoughts and convictions will show your sincerity and concern. Remember, you are the expert on libraries. Share your experiences.

4. Sign your full name and address so the legislator or other government official can reply to you.

5. Make your position clear. Say exactly what it is you wish the government official to do. If possible, refer to the issue you're writing about by its official title (such as "Senate Bill 259"). It is best to write about only one proposed law (bill) or issue in each letter.

6. Give your own personal experience to support your request. Tell briefly how the issue will affect you, your family, your library, or your community.

7. Ask the official to state his or her position on the issue in a reply to you.

8. Address the government official correctly. (Current address information for elected officials is found on your state legislature/county board/municipal council website.) Your letter should begin, "Dear Governor (or Senator) (or Representative) (last name)." Appointed officials are also addressed as "The Honorable _____," with "Mr. or Ms." as the correct title.

Source: Wisconsin Library Association with thanks to Citizens for Missouri's Children.

---

a library system, professional library association, or state library agency needs to step in and provide leadership.

Using resources available through the American Library Association, many public library systems in Wisconsin have developed "Speak Up for Your Library" advocacy lists. The primary goal is to educate the state's residents about the value of public libraries, and, in turn, to build a base of support that can be called upon when the need arises. More importantly, it provides a means of communicating with library patrons and mobilizing them on behalf of libraries at the local, regional, and state levels. Participation in this advocacy network is strictly voluntary. Library staff encourage patrons to sign up via a postcard registration form, prominently placed at service desks and popular browsing locations, to indicate their interest (see figure 7.1).

Members of the list receive general e-mails on a monthly basis, both as a way to share informative news about libraries and to determine the validity of the e-mail addresses. When the situation requires a call to action, the list can be tailored to respond to local, county, or statewide threats.

FIGURE 7.1 : Postcard registration form for "Speak Up
for Your Library" advocacy lists

Yes, I want to speak up for my library!

My library is important to me, so please send an e-mail when my library
needs help, or when libraries in general need my support. I am willing to
contact my elected officials to let them know how important library resources and services are to me and my family.

Name: _____

E-mail Address: _____
        –We will only contact you by email!–

Address: _____

City: _____ WI, ZIP Code_____
        Your mailing address will only be used for demographic purposes.

Library: _____

State Rep.: _____ State Sen.: _____

Sponsored by this library and the Indianhead Federated Library System.

KEEPING UP WITH LIBRARY ISSUES

Developing a conscientious program of professional reading is a surefire way to stay apprised
of and become better informed about library issues and trends. Immersing yourself in such a
program is an important part of the self-paced, independent learning aspect of your continuing
education and professional development. Think of this process as "environmental scanning," a
method of gathering information from both primary and secondary sources that describes how
internal factors (e.g., staff, library users) and external forces (e.g., technology, book publishing)
impact the library's operations.

A good starting point is a quartet of long-standing and well-respected periodicals that have
provided news and analysis on library and related topics for decades. In addition to their print
formats, all four have developed a strong web presence.

American Libraries, "the magazine of the American Library Association," is published
ten times per year. The subscription price is included in ALA member dues. In addition to its stated purpose as the association's official organ to provide "full and accurate information about the activities, purposes, and goals of the Association," *AL*

includes announcements, columns, news items, and feature-length stories about all types of libraries and all aspects of library services.

Library Journal, published twenty times per year, offers three feature stories per issue, plus commentary, technology news, extensive media coverage (including a column on gaming), collection development suggestions, "best" lists, and an extensive section of book, audiovisual, and professional reading reviews. *LJ's* website provides regularly updated links to the latest library news and blog posts.

Public Libraries, published six times per year, bills itself as "the only ALA journal devoted exclusively to public libraries." Each issue includes opinion pieces, "Tales from the Front" news items, Public Library Association news, new product news, reviews of professional literature, and timely feature articles. Past issues of *Public Libraries* are available online. Subscribe to the *PLA Blog* via an RSS feed for ongoing news and updates.

Publishers Weekly, as its website notes, has been around since 1872 and is considered "the book industry's leading news magazine." Although not targeted directly at a library audience, it is still essential reading for any director who wishes to keep pace with issues and trends concerning all formats in the publishing industry—book, audio, video, and electronic. Author interviews are a regular feature. In addition, each issue contains an extensive section of book and audiovisual media reviews.

The well-informed library director will also want to include the following items on a conscientious reading list:

Your local newspaper (While you're at it, introduce yourself to the editor and a reporter who is assigned to the local beat, if you haven't already done so.)

Your municipal council and county board meeting minutes (Your occasional attendance at these meetings is also encouraged.)

One or two major state newspapers (Choose a newspaper that provides comprehensive coverage of the state legislature and legislative issues.)

Library blogs (Learn what other libraries in your area or library system are doing. Focus on libraries whose service area population is similar.)

Your state library association's website, newsletter, and blog—whatever methods it uses to share information with its members (Be sure to share legislative alerts and advocacy messages with your local network of library supporters.)

Sources/calendars of continuing education (Continuing education programs designed to keep librarians up-to-date are offered by a variety of sources, including state library agencies, regional library systems and networks, ALA and its divisions, and schools of library and information studies. Many of these programs are now offered in formats that don't require travel to conferences or classrooms, such as online courses, webinars, and DVDs.)

NOTES

1. Wayne Senville, "Libraries at the Heart of Our Communities," *Planning Commissioners Journal,* no. 75 (Summer 2009): 12.
2. Peggy Barber and Linda Wallace, "Our Kind of Town: How the Chicago Public Library Is Changing the City," *American Libraries* (April 2007): 57.
3. Shari Gasper, "Downtown DeForest: A Decade of Change," *DeForest (WI) Times-Tribune,* February 10, 2010.
4. Neal Peirce, "Libraries Advance Against All Odds," http://citiwire.net/post/2215/.
5. American Library Association, "Frontline Advocacy Begins with You," http://www.ala.org/ala/issuesadvocacy/advocacy/advocacyuniversity/frontline_advocacy/intro.cfm.
6. American Library Association, *A Communications Handbook for Libraries,* www.ala.org/ala/aboutala/offices/pio/availablepiomat/online_comm_handbook.pdf.
7. Carl L. Cannon, *Publicity for Small Libraries* (Chicago: American Library Association, 1929).

INDEX

A

accountability (library finances), 35–37
accrual basis accounting, defined, 37
"achievement loss," 98
"across-the-desk" comments, 118
ad hoc committees, 6
Administration of the Small Public Library
(Weingand), 90
administrative structure and governance of libraries,
3–5
adult services, 98–100
advertising flyers, 114
advocacy for library, 126–132
ALA/Gates Foundation study, 66
Alice Baker Memorial Library (Wisconsin), 113
allocation decision accountability performance, 33
alternative funding
about, 25–26
corporate foundations versus giving programs, 25
fines and fees, 27–29
Friends of the Library groups, 26
grants, 27
library foundations, 26–27
American Libraries (journal), 104, 124, 132
American Library Association (ALA), 15, 85, 113,
127
American Sociological Review, 100
Americans with Disabilities Act (ADA), 41
"anchor store" concept, 125
annual report data, 36

appropriate behavior, defining, 13
appropriation, defined, 37
architect selection, 65
Article VI, Library Bill of Rights, 111
Association of Library Trustees, Advocates, Friends
and Foundations, 26, 128
audiobook selection criteria, 75

B

bad weather closing procedure, 60–61
Barber, Peggy, 126
Bettendorf (Iowa) Public Library, 31
blogs
keeping up with library issues, 133
public relations and, 117
board of trustees. *See* library boards
book collections. *See* collection management
book donations, 77–78
book groups, conducting, 100
Book Lust (Pearl), 105
books-by-mail service, 111
Broadus, Robert, 72–73
Brumback Library (Ohio), 2
budget hearings, 36
budgets
line-item, 31–33
preparing, 30–35
program, 33–35
reviewing, 35
summer reading program sample, 34

building program statement
    departmental descriptions,
        66–67
    design considerations, 66
    introductory statement, 65
    summary statement, 66
building systems malfunctions, 62
bulletin boards policy, 13
Buschman, John, 55
bylaws governing board of
        trustees, 6–7

C
Caplan, Audra, 126
cash basis accounting, defined, 37
censorship considerations, 86–87
Census Bureau, 20
Chicago Public Library, 124
Cihlar, Lisa, 99, 100
circulation policy, 12–13, 78–79, 82
circulation statistics, 19–20, 81
Citizen Request for
        Reconsideration of Library
        Materials form, 86
classes and informal instruction
    about, 106–109
    one-on-one instruction, 107–108
    public access computer stations,
        107
closing procedures, weather-
        related, 60–61
coaching sessions, 49
code of ethics, library board, 7
collection development policy,
        13, 86
collection management
    about, 71–73
    challenges to library materials,
        85–86
    circulation policy, 78–79
    collection evaluation, 79–85
    defined, 71
    development policy, 13, 86
    gifts, 77–78
    selection criteria, 73–77
    space considerations, 63
    weeding the collection, 81–83
collective bargaining agreements,
        51
Columbia University, 2
comment forms, 118–119
committee appointments, library
        board, 6
commons, library used as, 55
Communications Handbook for
        Libraries, 128

community center, library as, 55
community use of spaces
    exhibit space, 114
    meeting rooms, 111–114
community-centered philosophy,
        123–126
compensation package, 48
conservation versus preservation,
        85
construction, renovation,
        expansion
    architect selection, 65
    building program statement,
        65–66
    space considerations, 63–64
Cooper Union, 2
corporate foundations versus
        giving programs, 25
cost/demand relationship, 94–95
"Creating the Library Habit," 97
Crowley, Bill, 104

D
Dahlgren, Anders C., 63–64, 105
Daley, Richard M., 124
data collection (long-range
        planning), 19–20
"deferred giving," 27
DeForest (Wisconsin) Area Public
        Library, 47
DeForest (Wisconsin) Public
        Library, 124
DeForest Times-Tribune, 125
DelAWARE (online library), 2
Dempsey, Mary, 124
deposits and receipts (financial
        accountability), 35–36
developing library policies. See
        library policy development
Dewey Decimal classifications, 84
Dewey, Melvil, 2
disaster and emergency policies, 13
disciplinary policy, 43
discipline and grievances, 51–52
donated materials, 75–76
"double taxation," 29
Drake, Gloria, 31
Dwight Foster Public Library
        (Wisconsin), 29

E
earmarked funds (local funding),
        22
EBSCO Excellence in Small and/
        or Rural Public Library
        Service Award, 56

e-mail, public relations and, 118
emergency and disaster policies, 13
emergency closing procedure,
        61–62
Emergency Services Checklist, 60
Employee Withholding Allowance
        Certificate (W-4), 46
employees. See personnel
        management
encumbrance, defined, 37
equal employment opportunity
        policy, 43
equipment malfunctions, 62
evaluating
    collections, 79–85
    services and programs, 96–97
evaluation (planning document),
        19
executive summary (planning
        document), 16
exhibits policy, 13, 114, 116–117
expansion, renovation, new
        construction
    building program statement,
        65–66
    space considerations, 63–64
expenditure reports, 36–37
exterior signage, 57–58
external policies, 12

F
facilities
    access to technology, 66–69
    defining library spaces, 55–59
    Emergency Services Checklist,
        60
    renovation, expansion, new
        construction, 63–66
    safety issues, 59–63
Fair Labor Standards Act, 41
Famous First Facts, 112
federal and state aid (funding
        source), 23
financial management. See library
        finances
fines and fees (library finances),
        27–29, 31, 83
fire alarms, safety issues and, 61
Fletcher, Nancy, 113
focus groups, 119–120
foundations
    giving programs versus, 25
    grants and, 30
    library finances and, 26–27
Friends of the Library groups, 26,
        127–128

fund, defined, 37
funding sources
    additional and alternate
        funding, 25–30
    local funding, 21–22
    state and federal aid, 23–25

G

general fund (local funding), 22, 33
*Genreflecting: A Guide to Reading
    Interests in Popular Fiction,*
    105
Getting Out the Library Message
    checklist, 11
gifts, collection management and,
    77–78
gifts policy, 14
giving programs versus corporate
    foundations, 25
goals and objectives (planning
    document), 19
grants
    library finances and, 27
    sources of, 30
Grants to States program, 24
Green Lake (Wisconsin) Public
    Library, 26
Green, Samuel Swett, 104–105
grievance procedure, 43
grievances, discipline and, 51–52
group visits and tours policy, 14

H

Haines, Helen, 72
Harford County (Maryland) Public
    Library, 126
Hawaii State Public Library
    System, 24
health insurance policy, 42
Hennen's American Public Library
    Ratings, 28
hiring procedures, 44–46
holiday policy, 42
homebound delivery service, 111

I

I-9 forms, personnel records and,
    46
*Implementing for Results: Your
    Strategic Plan in Action,* 15
inappropriate behavior
    defining, 13
    safety issues, 62–63
Incident Report Template, 64
Institute of Museum and Library
    Services, 1, 3–4, 24, 98, 101

interior signage, 58–59
internal policies, 12
Internet use policy, 14
interviews, conducting, 45
introduction (planning document),
    16
Invitation to Serve Your Library
    template, 7
IRS 501(c)3 (non-profit status), 27
IRS Form 990, 25, 27

J

job descriptions
    library board, 8
    library staff, 41
jury duty policy, 42

K

kids' programs, 99
Kotler, Philip, 90

L

La Crosse (Wisconsin) Public
    Library, 99
Laird, Charlton, 129
laptops for in-library use, 68
leave of absence policy, 42
Leckie, Gloria J., 55
LeClaire (Iowa) Public Library, 31
legislators, writing and working
    with, 130–131
Lester Public Library (Wisconsin),
    98–99
"Libraries at the Heart of *Our
    Communities,*" 55, 124
library advocacy, 126–132
"Library Advocacy Now" web
    pages, 127
library as place
    developing community-
        centered philosophy,
        123–126
    keeping up with library issues,
        132–133
    library advocacy, 126–132
*The Library as Place: History,
    Community, Culture,* 55
Library Bill of Rights, 85–86, 111,
    114, 116
library boards (board of trustees)
    appointing committees, 6
    bylaws governing, 6–7
    citizen representation on, 5–6
    code of ethics, 7
    composition of, 5
    conducting meetings, 6

Getting Out the Library
    Message checklist, 11
Invitation to Serve Your Library
    template, 7
relationships between library
    directors and, 7–10
responsibilities of, 5, 9
sample job description, 8
library closings, weather-related,
    60–61
library, defined, 71
library directors
    Getting Out the Library
        Message checklist, 11
    need to know information for,
        40
    relationships between library
        boards and, 7–10
    responsibilities of, 9
    working with local officials,
        10–11
library finances
    accountability in, 35–37
    board of trustees and, 5
    budget preparation, 30–35
    budget review, 35
    funding sources, 21–30
    terminology for, 37
Library for the Blind and
    Physically Handicapped,
    113
Library Journal, 133
library materials, challenges to,
    86–87
library operations policy, 14
library policy development
    board of trustees and, 5
    bulletin boards policy, 13
    circulation policy, 12–13,
        78–79, 82
    collection development policy,
        13, 86
    defining inappropriate behavior,
        13
    emergency and disaster
        policies, 13
    exhibits policy, 13, 116
    gifts policy, 14
    group visits and tours policy, 14
    Internet use policy, 14
    library operations policy, 14
    meeting room policy, 12, 14,
        111–114
    outcomes of, 14
    personnel policies, 12, 14,
        40–44

library policy development (cont.)
  policies versus procedures, 12
  policy checklist, 13–14
  public notices policy, 13
  reference policy, 12, 14
  sample policies, 42–43
  service and program policies,
    12, 14
  study rooms policy, 14
  volunteers policy, 12, 14, 52–53
library programs. *See* services and
    programs
Library Services Act (1956), 2,
    25
Library Services and Construction
    Act (LSCA), 25
Library Services and Technology
    Act (LSTA), 24–25
library spaces
  defining, 55
  physical library, 56–59
  virtual library, 56
library staff. *See* personnel
    management
library tax (local funding), 22
line item, defined, 37
line-item budgets, 31–33
Living with Books (Haines), 72
local funding (library finances),
    21–22
local officials, library directors
    working with, 10–11
Loch-Wouters, Marge, 99
long-range planning
  data collection, 19–20
  library service roles and
    responses, 15–17, 90
  planning documents, 16–19
  planning timeline, 15, 18

M
Machine Readable Cataloging
    System (MARC), 2
maintenance-of-effort policy, 23
Mannix, Susan, 31
*Marketing for Nonprofit
    Organizations* (Kotler), 90
marketing services and programs,
    118
Martin, Rose, 76
McColvin, Lionel, 71
meeting room policy, 12, 14,
    111–115
Middleton (Wisconsin) Public
    Library, 7–9, 19, 28, 68,
    103
Minneapolis Public Library, 2

mission statement
  in planning document, 16
  sample, 19
Monona, Wisconsin signage, 58
morale, boosting staff, 52
Mortimer, Kirsten, 101
MUSTIE acronym, 81

N
National Center for Education
    Statistics (NCES), 103
newspaper selection criteria, 75
Nielsen, Steven, 31

O
Ohio College Library Center
    (OCLC), 2
open meeting laws, 6
outreach services, 109–111, 113
Overbeck, Nicole, 87

P
Pauline Haass Public Library
    (Wisconsin), 101, 113
Pearl, Nancy, 105
Peirce, Neal, 125
performance evaluations, 49–50
periodical selection criteria, 74, 75
personnel management
  boosting staff morale, 52
  classification and salary
    schedule, 42
  discipline and grievances,
    51–52
  employee benefits, 48–49
  employee compensation, 47–48
  extrinsic motivators, 50
  fringe benefits, 32–33
  Getting Out the Library
    Message checklist, 11
  hiring procedures, 44–46
  need to know information for
    staff, 40
  personnel policies, 14, 40–44
  personnel records, 46
  policies for, 12
  staff job descriptions, 41
  supervision, 49–50
  volunteers, 52–53
  work schedules, 46
"planned deterioration," 85
*Planning and Role Setting for
    Public Libraries: A Manual
    of Options and Procedures*,
    15, 55
Planning Commissioners Journal,
    55, 124

planning documents, 16–19
*Planning for Results: A Public
    Library Transformation
    Process*, 15, 55
*Planning for Results, the
    Guidebook: A Public
    Library Transformation
    Process*, 89
planning, long-range. *See* long-
    range planning
*A Planning Process for Public
    Libraries*, 15
planning timeline, 15, 18
policy development. *See* library
    policy development
preservation versus conservation,
    85
problem patrons, safety issues,
    62–63
procedures
  defined, 12
  library policies versus, 12
professional development policy,
    43
program budgets, 33–35
programs. *See* services and
    programs
promoting services and program,
    114–121
property taxes (local funding),
    22, 25
PTO (paid time off), 48
public libraries
  administrative structure and
    governance, 3–5
  defined, 1–2
  historical highlights, 2
  locations of, 3
  by population group, 3
  service roles and responses,
    15–17, 90
Public Libraries (journal), 133
Public Libraries and the Internet,
    66
*Public Libraries Survey: Fiscal
    Year 2007*, 25
*Public Library Space Needs: A
    Planning Outline/2009*, 63
public notices policy, 13
public relations, 115–118
Publishers Weekly (magazine), 133
purchase order, defined, 37
"pyramid effect," 97

R
radio, public relations, 116–117
Razzano, Barbara Will, 97

readers' advisory, 104–105
Reader's Guide, 109
real estate taxes, 22
receipts and deposits (financial accountability), 35–36
"Rediscovering the History of Readers Advisory Service," 104
reference interviews, elements of, 110
reference policy, 12, 14
reference services, 40, 100–104
renovation, expansion, new construction
  architect selection, 65
  building program statement, 65–66
  space considerations, 63–64
resignation and retirement policy, 43
retirement and resignation policy, 43
revenue reports, 36

S
safety issues
  about, 59
  bad weather closing procedure, 60–61
  building systems malfunctions, 62
  emergency closing procedure, 61–62
  equipment malfunctions, 62
  fire alarms, 61
  inappropriate behavior, 13, 62–63
  problem patrons, 62–63
Secure Rural Schools and Community Self-Determination Act, 23
Selecting Materials for Libraries (Broadus), 72
selection criteria
  for audiobooks, 74, 75
  for books, 74
  for periodicals, 74, 75
  for realia, 74
  sample criteria, 74
  for video/DVD, 74, 75
Senville, Wayne, 124
Sequels: An Annotated Guide to Novels in Series, 105
services and programs
  adult services, 98–100
  board of trustees and, 5
  books-by-mail service, 111
  budgets for, 33–35

building statements, 65–66
building teen services, 102–103
classes and informal instruction, 106–109
community use of space, 111–114
cost/demand relationship, 94–95
evaluating, 96–97
facility space considerations, 63–64
homebound delivery service, 111
identifying proper mix, 89–96
kids' programs, 99
long-range planning, 15
outreach services, 109–111, 113
policies for, 12, 14
promoting, 114–121
readers advisory, 104–105
reference services, 100–104
service roles and responses, 15–17, 90
setting priorities, 90–95
suggested cosponsors, 103
summer reading program, 34, 101
technology and, 105–106
youth services, 97–98
sick leave policy, 42
signage, facility, 57–59
social networks, public relations and, 118
"Speak Up for Your Library" advocacy lists, 131–132
staff. *See* personnel management
standing committees, 6
state and federal aid (funding source), 23
state library agency, 24
Strategic Planning for Results, 15
study rooms policy, 14
summer reading program, 34, 101
supervisory role, 49–50
SWOT analysis, 96–97

T
tax-deductible contributions, 27–28, 77–78
taxpayer "revolts," 25
technology access
  about, 66–68
  lending laptops for in-library use, 68
  library services and, 105–106
  technology competencies, 69
teen services, building, 102–103

television, public relations, 117
term limits, library board, 6
The Theory of Book Selection for Public Libraries (McColvin), 71
Thomas Memorial Library (Maine), 57
timelines, planning, 15, 18
title page (planning document), 16

U
U.S. Census Bureau, 20
U.S. Citizenship and Immigration Services (USCIS), 46
"user fees," 29

V
vacation policy, 42
Van Dan, Rebecca, 103
video/DVD selection criteria, 74, 75
virtual library, 56
volunteers policy, 12, 14, 52–53

W
W-4 (Employee Withholding Allowance Certificate), 46
"Walk Into the Library for the First Time" (activity), 56
Wallace, Linda, 126
Washington County (Maryland) Free Library, 2, 112
Washington Post, 125
Waukesha County (Wisconsin) Library System, 113
Wautoma (Wisconsin) Library, 87
weather-related closing procedures, 60–61
websites, public relations, 117
weeding the collection, 81–84
Weingand, Darlene E., 90
What Do I Read Next?, 105
Wisconsin Library Association, 130–131
word-of-mouth marketing (WOMM), 126
work schedule policy, 43
work schedules, 46

Y
"You Asked, We Listened" promotion, 118
youth services, 97–98

Z
zero-based budgeting, 33

You may also be interested in

LIBRARY MANAGEMENT 101:
A Practical Guide

Edited by Diane L. Velasquez

In addition to providing students with a solid foundation in library management, experienced managers will also benefit from the structured, practical knowledge included in this impressive volume.

PRINT: 978-0-8389-1148-8
448 PGS / 6" X 9"

STAFF DEVELOPMENT, 4E

EDITED BY CAROL ZSULYA, ANDREA STEWART, AND CARLETTE WASHINGTON-HOAGLAND FOR LLAMA

ISBN-13: 978-0-8389-1149-5

BE A GREAT BOSS

CATHERINE HAKALA-AUSPERK

ISBN-13: 978-0-8389-1068-9

PUBLIC LIBRARIES AND RESILIENT CITIES

EDITED BY MICHAEL DUDLEY

ISBN-13: 978-0-8389-1136-5

WORKPLACE LEARNING & LEADERSHIP

LORI REED AND PAUL SIGNORELLI

ISBN-13: 978-0-8389-1082-5

ORGANIZATIONAL STORYTELLING FOR LIBRARIANS

KATE MAREK

ISBN-13: 978-0-8389-1079-5

THE CHALLENGE OF LIBRARY MANAGEMENT

WYOMA vanDUINKERKEN AND PIXEY ANNE MOSLEY

ISBN-13: 978-0-8389-1102-0

Order today at **alastore.ala.org** or **866-746-7252!**
ALA Store purchases fund advocacy, awareness, and accreditation programs for library professionals worldwide.

CPSIA information can be obtained at www.ICGtesting.com
Printed in the USA
LVOW020806201111

255774LV00006B/2/P

9 780838 910856